NELSON

NELSON

~~Orazio Nelson of the Nile~~

Arthur Bryant

'He standeth in stone
Aloft and alone,
Riding the sky
With one arm and one eye.'
Robert Bridges

COLLINS/FONTANA

First published by Collins 1970
First issued in Fontana Books 1972
© Sir Arthur Bryant 1970

Printed in Great Britain
Love & Malcomson Ltd
Redhill, Surrey

CONTENTS

THE STATE OF THE NAVY

'If there is, indeed, a rot in the wooden walls
of old England, our decay cannot be very
distant.'

R. B. *Sheridan*

The Royal Navy had made its entry onto the world stage
under Drake and the Elizabethans, had sunk into insigni-
ficance under the early Stuarts, recovered under Crom-
well and the second Charles to wrest the sceptre of
ocean commerce from Holland, and, given administrative discipline by the life-long labours of Pepys, became
during the eighteenth century the leading arbiter of
human affairs at sea. Yet until the age of Nelson its
ascendancy was never undisputed. For over a hundred
years monarchical France, with its much greater population and resources, had contended with Britain for command of the sea and, on more than one occasion, all but
attained it. Britain's danger was greatest when France
and the Atlantic empire of Spain joined hands against
her, as they did during the American War, when, from
1778–83, with her fleets outnumbered, she had had to
fight for her very existence.

Yet Britain had always triumphed in the last resort
because the sea was her whole being, whereas with her
Continental rivals it was only a secondary consideration.
'The thing which lies nearest the heart of this nation,'
Charles II had written, 'is trade and all that belongs to
it.' Being an island, her commerce was maritime and its
protection an essential interest of an ever-growing num-

ber of her people. They were ready to make sacrifices
for the Navy which they would never have done for the
Army or any other service of the Crown. For it was on
the Navy, as the Articles of War put it, that under the
Providence of God the safety, honour, and welfare of
the realm depended.

Because of these things the Navy touched mystic
chords in the English heart which went deeper than
reason. The far sails of a frigate at sea, the sight of a
sailor with tarry breeches and rolling gait in any inland
town, and that chief of all the symbolic spectacles of
England, the Grand Fleet lying at anchor in one of her
white-fringed roadsteads, had for her people the power
of a trumpet call. So little Byam Martin, seeing for the
first time the triple-tiered ships of the line lying in
Portsmouth harbour, remained 'riveted to the spot, per-
fectly motionless, so absorbed in wonder' that he would
have stayed there all day had not his hosts sent a boat's
crew to fetch him away. From that hour his mind was
'inflamed with the wildest desire to be afloat.' Bobby
Shafto going to sea with silver buckles on his knee was
an eternal theme of eighteenth century England : of
such stuff were admirals made.

They had a hard schooling. Flung at twelve into
an unfamiliar world of kicks and cuffs, crowded hammocks and icy hardships, or after a few months under
'Black Pudding,' the omnipresent horsewhip of the
Naval Academy, Gosport, apprenticed as midshipmen to
the cockpit of a man-of-war, they learnt while still
children to be Spartans, dined off scrubbed boards on
salt beef, sauerkraut and black-strap, and became complete masters before they were men of a wonderful tech-
nical skill in all that appertained to the sailing and
fighting of ships.

They were as inured to roughness and salt water as gulls to wind. Boys in their teens would spend days afloat in the maintop, ready at any moment to clamber to the masthead when top-gallant or studding sail needed setting or taking in. They grew up like bulldogs, delighting to cuff and fight : in some ships it was the practice while the officers were dining in the wardroom for the midshipmen to engage regularly in pitched battles on the quarterdeck, Romans against Trojans, for the possession of the poop, banging away, 'all in good part,' with broomsticks, handswabs, boarding pikes and even muskets. Midshipman Gardner of the *Edgar*, being pinked in the thigh by a comrade with a fixed bayonet in the course of one of these friendly scraps, retaliated by putting a small quantity of powder into a musket and firing at his assailant, marking 'his phiz' for life. So toughened, they faced the world on their toes ready for anything and everyone. Such were the high-spirited midshipmen who pelted the British ambassador with plums at the Carnival at Pisa and, as he looked angry, hove another volley at his lady, observing that she seemed better tempered than his Excellency. So also the officers of the wardroom, dining at the best inn in Leghorn and growing somewhat merry, rolled the waiter among the dishes in the table-cloth and pelted the passers-by with loaves and chicken legs.

These were the permanent cadre of the Navy; the officers of the establishment, 'born in the surf of the sea,' who, unlike the lower deck, coming and going as occasion demanded, lived in the Service and died in it. They were bound together by the closest of professional honour, etiquette and experience. Socially they were of all sorts : one high-born captain filled his frigate with so many sprigs of aristocracy that his first lieutenant—no respecter of persons—was wont to call out in mockery to the young noblemen and honourables at the ropes, 'My lords and gentlemen, shiver the mizen topsail!' The majority were of comparatively humble origin, occasioning Sir Walter Elliot's remark in Jane Austen's *Persuasion* that, though the profession had its utility, he would be sorry to see any friend of his belonging to it. Few had much of this world's goods nor, unless exceptionally lucky over prize money, could hope for much. Some were scholars—for it was a literary age—and read their Shakespeare or discoursed learnedly on the classical associations of the foreign ports they visited : more often they were simple souls, 'better acquainted with rope-yarns and bilge water than with Homer or Virgil.' But one and all were masters of their profession, proud in their obedience to king and country and ready to give their lives and all they had whenever the Service demanded. 'A bloody war and a sickly season!' was the closing toast of many a jovial evening in the wardroom : it was so that men rose in their calling.

Such men not only officered the fleet : they gave it their own tone and spirit. They were often rough teachers, full of fearful oaths like the master's mate of the *Edgar* who ended every sentence with a 'Damn your whistle,' and too fond of enforcing their commands with the lash. But the men they commanded were rough too; hard-bitten merchant seamen and fishermen, brought into the Service for the duration by the pressgangs, with always a sediment in every ship of jailbirds and incorrigibles whose only chance of freedom was the hard life of the sea. The unresting, automatic discipline which the handling of wind-propelled warships in northern waters demanded could not have been enforced by gentler souls : it was that which gave Britain command of the waves and kept the Royal Navy from the slovenly, helpless degradation which befell that of revolutionary France. From the admiral, piped on board, to the boatswain's mate with his colt ready to 'start' the lower deck to action, strictly ordered subordination and readiness to obey were the hallmarks of the Service.

The life of the seamen was a life apart; something that was of England and yet remote from it. A king's ship was a little wooden world of its own, with its peculiar customs and gradations unguessed at by landsmen; its proud foretopmen, the aristocrats of the sea, and far down out of sight its humble waisters: pumpers and sewermen, scavengers and pigsty keepers. In such a community, often years together away from a home port, men learnt to know each other as they seldom can on shore: to love and trust, to fear and hate one another. There were ships that became floating hells, ruled by some sadistic tyrant, with drunken, flogging officers 'crabbed as fiends,' and savage, murderous crews such as that which flung Bligh of the *Bounty* to perish in an open boat in a remote sea. There were others commanded by captains like Nelson, Pellew and Duncan, where the men looked on their officers as fathers and were eager to dare and do anything for them. Here something of the unspoken sympathy between experienced rider and horse entered into the relationship between quarter and lower deck.

The nation honoured its rough, simple seamen, as it had cause to, though it usually saw them at their worst: ashore on their brief spells of leave, with discipline relaxed and their hard-earned money riotously dissipated on brandy and the coarse Megs and Dolls of the seaports. But it saw too, as we also can glimpse from the prints of the old masters, the fine manly faces, the earnest gaze, the careless attitudes so full of strength and grace for all the gnarls and distortions of weather, accident and disease : symbols of rugged-headed courage, manly devotion and simple-hearted patriotism. They were children—generous, suspicious, forgiving, with the fortitude and patience of men : rough Britons tempered by the unresting sea into virtue of a rare and peculiar kind. The sight of a Monsieur's sails roused in them all the unconquerable pugnacity of their race : the whine of Johnny Crapaud's shot whipped their quick tempers to savagery. Though chivalrous and generous victors, they were not good losers like the courtly Spaniards and the aristocrats of the old French navy; they had to beat their adversary or die. As they waited at quarters before a fight, 'their black silk handkerchiefs tied round their heads, their shirt-sleeves tucked up, the crows and handspikes in their hands and the boarders all ready with their cutlasses and tomahawks,' they reminded an eye-witness of so many devils.

Yet from such scenes the British sailor could pass in a few hours to the buffoonery and practical jokes dear to the lower deck, the fiddler's lively air, the droll or pathetic ballads with their rhythm of the waves, while the seas broke over the forecastle and the ship pitched and rolled; and to those tenderer moments when, homeward bound, hearts panted with the anticipated happiness of meeting wives and sweethearts and the head-wind's moping contrariness was lulled by the chorus of 'Grieving's a folly, Boys!'

> *'And now arrived that jovial night*
> *When every true bred tar carouses,*
> *When, o'er the grog, all hands delight*
> *To toast their sweethearts and their spouses.'*

History loves to linger over the good-humoured jollity between decks when port was reached : the girls on the seamen's knees with sturdy, buxom arms around their necks; the reels and gigs as Susan's bright eyes promised her Tom Tough his long-awaited reward; the grog and flip that passed about under the light of the flickering lanterns. And judging by the popularity of Dibdin's songs, the nation liked to think of such scenes too and took deep comfort in the thought of the hearts of oak and jolly tars that kept its foes at bay.

.   .   .

In 1797—the fifth year of Britain's struggle against the militant power of Revolutionary France—the Royal Navy alone stood between her and defeat. One by one her continental allies had collapsed before the élan of the ragged revolutionary armies; Prussia and Holland had given up the fight and entered the enemy camp, Piedmont had sued for an armistice, and, in the autumn of 1796, the sudden defection to the French cause of Spain and its powerful navy—lying athwart Britain's trade and ocean communications—had forced her to withdraw her fleet from the Mediterranean, where that summer a young general named Napoleon Bonaparte had overrun northern Italy in a series of dazzling victories over her ally, Austria. The three chief naval powers of the continent—France, Spain and Holland—were now aligned against her, outnumbering her ships of the line by nearly two to one. Ireland was on the verge of revolution, the working-class population of the industrial north was hungry and restless, and powerful invasion-forces were waiting with transports at Brest and Texel for a chance to break the blockade and strike at England or Ireland. During the last fortnight of 1796, the Brest expedition got to sea and reached the Irish coast, only to be driven back by gales; in February, after an abortive attempt to burn Bristol, a raiding force made landings on either side of the Bristol Channel, causing a panic in the City, during which Pitt's Government suspended cash payments and seemed about to fall. Only a timely victory off Cape St. Vincent on St. Valentine's Day over a Spanish fleet gave the country a respite.

But nine weeks later, on the morning of April 17th, dreadful rumours began to percolate through the capital. The Navy, which had saved the country from invasion, was about to betray it to its enemies. The Channel Fleet—the buckler on which England's very existence depended—had refused to sail and mutinied for an increase of pay. By nightfall the news was confirmed. And at that very moment the Austrians were on the point of asking a truce from the victorious Bonaparte, Ireland—almost denuded of troops—was defenceless, and a French army of liberation was waiting to embark at the Texel under cover of the Dutch fleet. Like the Black Death four centuries before, the Revolution had crossed the Channel and broken out in England.

•   •   •

Naval pay, fixed by ancient enactment, had stood for nearly a century and a half at 10s. a month for an ordinary seaman and 24s. for an A.B. But the price of the commodities on which the sailor's family depended had not remained constant. To the normal rising trend of prices had been added war inflation, now aggravated by a bank crisis. In the merchant service the laws of supply and demand had raised the seaman's pay to four times the naval rate. Prevented by the pressgang from selling their highly skilled services in the open market and forced to let their wives and children starve while they served their country, the men of the Royal Navy were conscious of a grave injustice of which their rulers—ill-served by statistics—were blissfully unaware. Even the despised soldiers had been given a small rise since the war. But the sailors—the pride and defence of the nation—had had nothing done for them, though certain of their officers had recently had increases. So strong was their feeling that at the beginning of March before sailing for the spring cruise the men of the Channel Fleet combined to send round-robins to old Lord Howe, their nominal commander-in-chief. In these they respectfully pointed out that the cost of living had doubled and that their pay was insufficient to support their families. And since it was only paid in the port of commission, whence in war-time a ship might be absent for months and even years, it was frequently in arrears.

As Howe was an invalid at Bath and about to hand over his command finally to his deputy, Lord Bridport, he merely forwarded the petitions to the Admiralty. Here they were ignored. For in the critical state of the country's finances, application to parliament for a rise in naval pay seemed out of the question, and discussion of the matter would thus obviously be undesirable. As the petitions were anonymous no reply was made. When the fleet returned to Spithead at the end of March the men found their request met by silence. They were very angry and took steps to prepare a petition to parliament and to support it by joint action. 'They had better,' the *Queen Charlotte*'s men wrote of the Government, 'go to war with the whole globe than with their own subjects.'

Of all this Lord Bridport was unaware. For through an administrative oversight the Admiralty had failed to inform him of the petitions. But on April 12th he acci-

dentally learnt of a plot to seize the ships and hold them
as pledges for redress of grievances. He was naturally
profoundly shocked and, hearing at second hand of the
petitions to Howe, became exceedingly indignant with
the Admiralty. In his heart he sympathised with the
men's demands. But when he raised the matter with
Whitehall he was merely told to take the Fleet to sea.
For the Admiralty was determined to sidetrack the
matter.

On the morning, therefore, of April 16th—Easter
Sunday—Bridport reluctantly ordered the Fleet to weigh
anchor. His signal was ignored. In the *Queen Charlotte*,
Howe's former flagship, the men, seeing an attempt to
forestall the mutiny, manned the shrouds and gave
three cheers—the pre-arranged signal for revolt. At
once the leaders put off in boats and rowed round the
fleet, ordering the crew of every vessel to send two delegates that night to the *Queen Charlotte*. Like all the
Hoods a shrewd and sensible man, Bridport forbade his
captains to resist. Instead he ordered them to muster
their men and ask them to state their grievances.

That evening the delegates of sixteen battleships
assembled in the *Queen Charlotte*'s state-room to draw
up rules for the regulation of the fleet. They ordered
watches to be kept, drunkenness to be punished by flogging and ducking, and yard-ropes to be rove at every
fore-yard arm to enforce their authority. Women were
to be allowed aboard as usual in harbour, but to prevent
tittle-tattle were not to go ashore till the matter was
settled. Respect was to be paid to the rank of officers,
but, until the desires of the men were satisfied, not an
anchor was to be raised. To symbolise their unanimity
the shrouds were to be manned morning and night and
three cheers given.

It was a strange position. The fleet was in indubitable mutiny. Yet the men did not regard themselves as mutineers and persisted in trying to behave as though ordinary discipline prevailed. The country was at war with an ideological creed which glorified revolution : it was hourly expecting invasion. Yet in the rebellious ships there was no sign of sympathy with that revolution : on the contrary the delegates declared that the fleet would sail at once if the French put to sea. They even stopped the frigates and small craft from taking part in the mutiny lest the country's trade should suffer. Nervous folk on shore, imagining 'secret Jacobin springs,' looked for foreign agents and agitators. But if there were any such, they were unsuccessful in impressing their principles on their old foes of the Channel Fleet. In its good order, common sense and almost pathetic legalism the start of the English revolution contrasted strangely with the French.

Meanwhile Admiral Pole, dispatched post-haste with news of the mutiny, had reached the Admiralty at midnight on the 16th. In the small hours of Tuesday morning he told his horrifying story to the First Lord. Earl Spencer was the best type of patrician—an athlete still in early middle age, a scholar with liberal leanings, red-haired and handsome. He acted with promptitude and vigour. As soon as it was light he hurried to the Prime Minister and, after a day of interviews, set out for Portsmouth with two junior Lords and the Secretary of the Admiralty.

Here on the 18th the Board, formally sitting in the Fountain Inn, opened its proceedings. Refusing to compromise its dignity by meeting the seamen personally, it used the flag officers of the fleet as go-betweens. It might have been wiser for Spencer, who was over-per-

suaded by his Service colleagues, to have settled the
matter directly with the delegates, whose real weakness
was not Jacobinism but excessive suspicion. As it was,
in the delays and second thoughts born of too much
coming and going, the seamen's conditions tended to
rise. A new petition added demands that rations—on
paper a pound of meat, a pound of biscuits and half a
pint of rum a day—should no longer be subjected to the
purser's customary deduction of an eighth, that fresh
vegetables should be provided in port, that the sick
should be properly cared for, that pay should be continued to the wounded until discharged, and that in
harbour men should have leave to go ashore instead of
remaining aboard like prisoners. The unknown hand
who framed this document asked that the sailors should
be looked upon as a number of men standing in the
defence of their country, and that they might in some
wise 'have the grant of those sweets of Liberty on shore
when in harbour.' He ended by assuring the Admiralty
that the men would suffer double the hardships they
complained of sooner than allow the Crown to be
imposed on by a foreign Power.

The new requests were in themselves reasonable : they
were all in the end granted without doing the country
the least injury. Pursers who 'took care of their eighths'
were far too common : the meat was often uneatable,
the biscuits weevily, the butter rancid and the cheese
full of long red worms.[1] Many ship's surgeons were

1. It was an old saying in the Service that Judas Iscariot was
the first purser. But boatswains often ran them fine in the art of
peculation. It was Johnny Bone, the boatswain of the *Edgar*, to
whom the great Adam Duncan observed : 'Whatever you do Mr.
Bone, I hope and trust you will not take the anchors from the
bows.' *Recollections of J. A. Gardner* (Navy Records Society), 71.

drunken wastrels who had gone to sea as the last resort in a life of professional failure. And considering that the seamen had been torn away from their homes and callings to indescribable hardships and tedium, it seemed monstrously unjust to keep them on board in harbour.

But, however reasonable, the ultimatum was presented at a time when the country was in graver danger than any since the Spanish Armada. To yield unconditionally at the pistol's mouth might undermine the whole fabric of naval discipline and precipitate the same tragic train of events which had brought monarchical France to massacre and ruin. To aristocrats like Spencer the very discipline of the mutineers seemed ominous: it argued, as Lady Spencer wrote to 'weathercock' Windham, a steadiness which overpowered her with terror. Therefore, though the Board prudently eschewed violent counsels, it determined to make some sort of a stand: to keep the seamen at a distance and, while granting the substance of their demands, to make as many minor abatements as possible. In fact it tried to avoid paying the full price for its own former and very English failure—through complacency, inertia and reluctance to inquire too closely into uncomfortable facts—to reform abuses while it had time to do so with dignity.

The results of this obstinacy were not happy. On the 20th the Prince of Wurtemberg, who had come to Portsmouth to marry the Princess Royal, had been cheered and saluted as though nothing unusual was happening while being escorted by Spencer round the mutinous fleet. This singularly English episode encouraged the Lords of the Admiralty in their firm resolve. But next day, while Admiral Gardner was arguing with the delegates in the *Queen Charlotte*'s stateroom, the men—after seeming agreement had been reached—grew suspicious and declared that a final settlement must wait till a pardon had been received under the king's hand. At this the admiral, who thought it high time the fleet was at sea, lost his temper and denounced the delegates as 'a damned, mutinous, blackguard set' of 'skulking fellows' who were afraid of meeting the French. In his fury he even shook one of them and threatened to have him hanged. At this there was a riot which ended in the apoplectic old man's being hustled out of the flagship and the red flag being hoisted in all ships. The officers were placed under confinement or—in the case of the unpopular ones—sent ashore.

Once more, faced by urgent crisis, Spencer acted promptly. That night he set out for London to obtain the royal pardon, secured next morning an immediate Cabinet council and by midnight had obtained the king's signature at Windsor and had had copies printed for circulation in the fleet. But by the time that these, galloped through the night, reached Portsmouth, the good temper of the Navy was already re-asserting itself. The astonishing delegates, while still insisting on the redress of grievances, had apologised gracefully to Bridport for the flag striking incident and begged him as 'father of the fleet' to resume command. This the admiral did on the morning of the 24th, reading the royal proclamation to the crew of the flagship and making a speech in which he promised general satisfaction of all demands. The mutiny thereupon ended. Next morning the greater part of the fleet dropped down to St. Helens to await an easterly wind to carry it to Brest.

But though the country congratulated itself that a dreadful week had been attended by no worse consequences, suspicion and unrest remained. The men were not sure that the Government meant to honour its

promises. The inexplicable delays attendant on parliamentary processes increased their distrust. During the
next fortnight while the fleet waited for the wind, the
ferment continued to work. The seamen had tasted
power and learnt their strength. Moreover the recognition of their principal grievances had reminded them
of others.

On several occasions in the recent past abuses in par-
ticular ships had been so serious that they had provoked
isolated mutinies. Over-rapidity of war-time expansion
and the difficulty of raising men and keeping them from
desertion had aggravated the severity of discipline. With
the jails emptied to supply the pressgangs, it is not sur-
prising that some officers could only enforce order at the
cat's tail. Such a regimen could be accompanied by a
horrible brutality. 'The ill-usage we have on board this
ship,' the crew of the *Winchelsea* wrote to the Admiralty
early in the war, 'forced us to fly to your Lordships the
same as a child to its father.' Another ship's company
referred to its treatment 'from the tirant of a captain' as
more than the spirits and hearts of Englishmen could
bear, 'for we are born free but now we are slaves.' These
things were against the Regulations, but, with each ship
a world of its own and often far from port, the Regulations were hard to enforce. In certain ships the officers,
as Collingwood said, beat the men into a state of insubordination.

Grievances apart, the Fleet was ripe for trouble. The
dilution of the better elements with the worse had left a
dangerous sediment at the bottom of every crew. In four
years of war naval personnel had swollen from 16,000 to
120,000. Many of the latest joined were 'quota men'
raised under the Act of 1795 which had imposed on
every parish the obligation of supplying the Service.

Among these were inevitably some of superior station—broken-down tradesmen, fraudulent attorneys and the like, who were disgruntled with their lot. Ten per cent of the seamen were foreigners. Another ten per cent were Irish, some of them under sentence for political offences and illegally smuggled into the Fleet by high-handed officials. Recently an increasing number had been United Irishmen and sympathisers with the principles proclaimed by revolutionary France.

The agitation and struggle of those seven breathless days at Spithead stirred all this perilous matter into a ferment. This was no ordinary mutiny, for it had succeeded. Suspicion that its fruits were going to be filched by parliamentary chicanery was now aroused by two circumstances. On May 3rd the Duke of Bedford, making party capital out of a national misfortune, contrived by an awkward question in the Lords to convey to uninitiated seamen poring over their newspapers the false idea that the Government was going to drop the bill for supplementary naval pay. Simultaneously the Admiralty circulated a foolish document forbidding captains to temporise with mutiny, and directing the marines to be kept in constant readiness for action. This was no more than a childish attempt of official pride to recover official face. But by accident or design its contents became known to the fleet. On Sunday, May 7th, when on a change of wind Bridport hoisted the signal to sail, the seamen at St. Helens once more manned the shrouds and broke into defiant cheers.

This time mutiny wore a graver aspect. The seamen of the *Royal George*, swearing their officers had deceived them, seized the arms and ammunition. A broil in Admiral Colpoys's flagship at Spithead, in which a seaman lost his life while rushing the quarterdeck, nearly ended in the admiral and the officer who had fired the shot being summarily hanged. In other ships unpopular officers were bundled ashore and left with their belongings on the quayside. Some of the marines, the traditional keypins of naval discipline, joined the rest. The people of Portsmouth, confronted with the spectacle of the fleet flying the red flag and of shaken captains and admirals dumped on the sea front like *émigrés*, hourly expected the arrival of the French and the guillotine. As a Civil Lord of the Admiralty wrote to Spencer, the situation formed 'the most awful crisis' the country had ever known.

Meanwhile the conflagration had spread. At Plymouth the crews of Sir Roger Curtis's squadron had mutinied on April 26th and turned most of their captains ashore. Four days later ominous cheering signalled an outbreak of revolt in the flagship of the North Sea Fleet waiting at Yarmouth for a wind to blockade the Dutch invasion fleet in the Texel. But in this case the admiral in command was equal to the occasion. Towering with rage, the giant Scot, Adam Duncan, called his men out of the foreshrouds and rated them like a father. The affair ended—for they adored the fine old man—in their promising to go to any part of the world with him and writing a letter thanking the Lords of the Admiralty for their compliance with the request of the Channel Fleet.

For underneath the suspicion, the smouldering grievances and agitation ran the English individual sense of humanity. A worthy officer remained in the seamen's eyes a worthy man, however much he might theoretically embody the forces of despotism. All the generalisations of French ideology or Irish logic could not persuade them otherwise.

It was this deep-rooted manliness of the British sailor

that saved the day. The authorities, at last abandoning
false pride, behaved with equal good sense. The supplementary estimates providing for the increase in pay were
hurried through their remaining stages, and the one line
of approach to the disgruntled seamen which was certain of success—the simple human one—was chosen.
Someone with a flash of the inspiration which always
seems to come to the salvation of England in the last
ditch suggested the victor of the First of June as *deus ex
machina*. Armed with full powers to redress grievances
on behalf of the Admiralty and to grant pardon on that
of the Crown, Lord Howe, overcoming gout and in-
firmities, set off for Portsmouth. Without wasting a
minute he had himself rowed across the Solent to St.
Helens where, visiting every ship in turn, he set to work
to restore the confidence of the seamen in their rulers.

By May 13th, six days after the renewed mutiny had
begun, the old hero had achieved his purpose of quieten-
ing what he described as 'the most suspicious but most
generous minds' he had ever met. The demand of the
men to dismiss the more unpopular officers was tactfully
turned by getting the latter to petition the Admiralty
for transfer to other ships. There only remained to celebrate the reconciliation of Fleet and nation. On May
15th, after twelve hours of rowing round the cheering
fleet amid the strains of 'Rule Britannia,' 'Black Dick'—
as exhausted as after the battle of the First of June—
was carried by the sailors shoulder high to the port
governor's house. Here in a perfect delirium of patriotic
emotion he and his lady entertained the delegates to a
grand dinner and jollification. At Plymouth, where a
similar happy ending occurred, Captain Boger, after
being kept a prisoner in the *Cambridge* guardship, was
paraded with his fellow captains in open carriages round

the town on a broiling summer day, amid tumultuous cheering. Dressed in full uniform, with a face scarlet from the heat, he repeatedly asked for a glass of water, but his men, who were extremely fond of him, horrified at the request, told him that 'his Honour might have any sort of grog, but that as for water they would not suffer his Honour to drink it.'

.   .   .

Two days later the Channel Fleet put to sea to seek the enemy. But the country had no time for relief. During the second Spithead mutiny the news reached London that Austria, brought to her knees by Bonaparte's advance on Vienna, had signed an armistice at Leoben and that France was free to concentrate her entire force against England. Already a Dutch army was waiting at the Texel. Every day brought new alarms. On May 12th, while Howe was completing his work of pacification, a brilliant young Tory M.P., George Canning, penned some mock verses congratulating his friend Windham, who had made a comforting ministerial reference in a recent speech to 'negative successes,' on a 'day of no disaster.' He was too soon. For on that very day, while rumours percolated through London that the Household troops had revolted, the men of the flagship at Sheerness defied their officers and turned the forecastle guns on the quarterdeck. The rest of the battleships lying in the mouth of the river at the Great and Little Nore followed their example.

The good humour and sense which had characterised proceedings at Spithead were lacking at the Nore. The chief ringleader was an ex-schoolmaster who had recently taken the Government's quota money to get himself out of a debtor's prison. The son of an Exeter tradesman, Richard Parker, now thirty years of age, had been three times to sea, had served as a midshipman and had been courtmartialled for insubordination. He marked his return to the Navy by helping to stir up trouble in the port flag and depot ship, the *Sandwich*, already rife with discontent through her foul and over-crowded condition. Like many other famous talkers he was full of good intentions, on which later apologists have dwelt at length. But he was without moral ballast. He was ambitious, vain, untruthful, weak and so excit-able as to seem at times mentally deranged. In his hands the smouldering grievances and resentment of rough and ignorant men became a terrible menace.

The mutineers at the Nore formulated no specific demands. It was mutiny without an objective. It dis-regarded the general settlement reached at Spithead. Like the French Revolution in miniature, it proceeded on its own momentum and degenerated into rebellion for the sake of rebellion. Parker, who styled himself President and kept up an admiral's state, never stirred without the accompaniment of musical honours and banners. He told the men that the act for the increase of their pay was only a temporary Order in Council and, when shown to be wrong, declared that it had no validity beyond the end of the year. Only after repeated requests for the men's grievances did he present Admiral Buckner—in whose presence he remained contemp-tuously covered—with an ultimatum of eight articles. One of these affirmed the right of seamen to dismiss their officers. But he refused to discuss matters with any one but the Lords of the Admiralty, insisting that they should wait on the delegates.

Meanwhile his followers ceaselessly paraded the streets of Sheerness or rowed in procession round the port, armed with pistols and cutlasses and accompanied by brass bands playing 'Rule Britannia' and 'Britons, Strike Home!' For the men, though greatly enjoying their holiday and unwonted power, Englishwise refused to admit any disloyalty in their attitude. When the Government marched two regiments of militia into the place, Parker wrote to Admiral Buckner protesting at the 'insult to the peaceable behaviour of the seamen.' He added that the Lords of the Admiralty were themselves remiss in their duty in failing to attend where their appearance would give satisfaction.

As the Admiralty declined to obey, the mutineers proceeded to more vigorous measures. On May 23rd, they seized eight gunboats lying in Sheerness harbour and carried them off in triumph to the Nore. Next day they dispatched delegates to Yarmouth to urge the men of the North Sea Fleet to join them. Here Admiral Duncan, having received news that the Dutch fleet was embarking for Ireland, was about to sail for the Texel. Though the fatal infection was at work in his ships, he trusted to his personal popularity to overcome it. Only a week before he had dealt with a further outbreak in the *Adamant* by hoisting his flag in her and asking the turbulent crew whether any man dared to dispute his authority. When one of the ringleaders said he did, the giant admiral had picked him up by the collar with one hand and, bearing him to the side of the vessel, had cried out, 'My lads, look at this fellow who dares to deprive me of the command of the fleet!' After which incipient mutiny in that ship at least dissolved in laughter.

But on the 29th, while standing out for the Dutch coast, one after another of Duncan's ships left him and sailed home to the Nore. Only his flagship, the *Venerable*, and the now faithful *Adamant* kept their course. 'I am sorry,' wrote the gallant old man, 'that I have lived to see the pride of Britain disgrace the very name of it.' Not since an enemy sailed up the Medway had such shame befallen the Navy.

Meanwhile on the evening of the 27th the Cabinet, faced by the gravity of the situation, resolved that the Admiralty must swallow its pride and go down to Sheerness. A new Royal Pardon was made out specifically covering the post-Spithead mutinies. That night Spencer, accompanied by two colleagues and the Secretary of the Board, again set off on his travels. But on reaching Sheerness on the 28th, he found what he had already suspected, that the Fleet's attitude was not unanimous and that many of the men were already sickening of Parker's presumption. He therefore refused to receive the delegates and, remaining in the Dockyard Commissioner's house, used old Admiral Buckner as an intermediary. And as Parker refused to abate anything from his demands, the First Lord presently returned to London with his mission unaccomplished. With Parker to deal with, it is doubtful if any other course was ever possible.

It was now war to the knife. Neither side would admit of compromise. While the mutineers were enthusiastically welcoming Duncan's absconding battleships, the Government was giving orders to cut their communications with the shore. All fraternisation between the Fleet and the Army was stopped and the sailors were to be resisted by force if they attempted to land. A bill was hurried through parliament extending the death penalty to persons having intercourse with rebellious seamen. Finally the provisions of the fleet at the Nore were stopped. These measures, which passed both Houses with only one dissentient vote, were stern in the extreme.

But they reflected the mood of the nation. They were
an instance of the English method of grappling with a
problem only when it became unmistakably dangerous
but then doing so without second thoughts or hesitation.
For the rulers of England weakness was a thing of the
past.

Nor did they stand on pride. The Army, whose loyalty
was so vital in that hour, was treated with a new consideration. Increases in pay long asked for in vain by the
military authorities were immediately granted by parliament. The soldiers responded cheerfully : having been
so often sneered at by the seamen for their inefficiency
and defeats, it was a pleasant change to become the
heroes of the nation and be set to police the proud
favourites. Under the command of Sir Charles Grey,
the most popular officer in the Army, the troops kept
close watch along the Kent and Essex shores and
scarcely allowed a man to pass.

Behind them was the nation. Its patriotism and sense
of danger were alike aroused : fear of the invader waiting at the Texel and the intangible bogey of revolution
that had grown up during the horrors of the Terror and
the unreasoning years of war propaganda. To simple
Britons Fox and his gang of Whig 'traitors' and
defeatists lurked under the delegates' table in the state-
room of the *Queen Charlotte*. To frustrate their vile
tricks and save the nation, thousands of middle-class
citizens enrolled as 'peace officers' or volunteered to
serve in the flotilla of gunboats which Commodore
Gower was organising in Long Reach to defend London
from the mutineers. The East India Company placed all
its ships at the Government's disposal : hundreds of
private merchants followed its example.

The stoppage of the fleet's victuals put the delegates in a quandary. Since they would not go back, they had to go forward. On May 31st they decided to 'show the country that they had it in their power to stop the trade of the river.' But when on June 2nd they did so, seizing every ship entering or leaving the Thames, they merely united the country more vigorously than before. The trading community, attacked at its most sensitive point, was appalled and, because it was appalled, furious. So were the good people of the Thames-side towns who found tarred and feathered officers dumped by piratical crews on their waterfronts. This was plainly the prelude to the orgy of massacre, rape and arson which the anti-Jacobin cartoonists had taught them to fear. When the Government retaliated against the blockade by removing the buoys and beacons at the mouth of the Thames, there was not a dissentient voice from a seafaring people.

As the rest of the nation became more unanimous, the seamen became less so. The mutiny was popular so long as it remained a holiday demonstration with plenty of triumphal processions ashore, patriotic songs and brass bands and an unwonted freedom for airing grievances and slighting tyrannical officers. It became another thing altogether when it meant being cooped in idle ships, denied the liberty of the shore and its taverns and kept to short commons. But what really sapped the spirit of mutiny was the realisation that the nation, which, however sparing it might be in other things, had always lavished unstinted praise on its sailors, now regarded them as traitors and French dupes. Even their brethren of Spithead and Plymouth, now returned to their allegiance, wrote to the men of the Nore expressing horror at their proceedings. This imputation was more than the sailors could bear. The sense of community and playing for one's side, so strong in Englishmen, kept them a little while longer loyal to the mutiny, but they became moody, suspicious of one another and openly critical of their leaders. 'Dam my eyes,' wrote one of them in desperation to a silent, unrelenting Admiralty, 'if I understand your lingo or long Proclimations, but in short give us our Due at Once and no more at it, till we go in search of the Rascals the Eneymes of our Country.' In such a mood their attempts to celebrate Oakapple Day and the king's birthday on June 5th, which struck their compatriots as an impertinence, assumed a pathetic significance.

On June 6th the Government formally declared the mutineers rebels, though still extending its offer of pardon to all who should submit except the ringleaders. About the same time it became known in the fleet that Parker had been keeping back the terms of this offer from his followers. Discontent at his admiral's airs and peremptory ways had been growing for some time : it now turned to open murmuring. The more popular officers detained aboard the ships were quick to take advantage of the change of temperature, and sober seamen who had never approved of the mutiny began to come into their own.

The first sign of collapse came on the morning of the 9th when Parker, sensing the altered mood of the men and desperately resolving to take the hungry fleet over to the Texel, gave the order to put to sea. Not a vessel stirred. The mutiny had come full circle. On the same day the officers of the *Leopard* seized control of the ship from the divided and disillusioned crew and set sail for the Lower Hope. The example was at once followed by the *Repulse* and, despite a desultory fire from the rest of the fleet, both ships made good their escape.

For the next few days the fleet presented a curious spectacle to watchers from the shore as red, blue and white flags fluttered up and down the mastheads while the ships' companies contended whether they should return unconditionally to their allegiance, make new attempts to parley with a stony-hearted Admiralty or sail for America or Ireland. But all the while the sands of mutiny were running out. The Admiralty refused to consider any proposition short of unqualified submission, and the men knew they had no alternative but to submit. By the 12th only two out of the twenty-two ships still at the Nore flew the red flag of defiance. Every day more of them slipped their cables and made their way up river to surrender to the authorities.

On the 15th the crew of the *Sandwich* repudiated Parker's authority and sailed under the guns of Sheerness. The mutiny was over. A few of the ringleaders made their escape to Calais. Parker, handed over to the military by his comrades, was taken to Maidstone jail under an escort of the West Yorks Militia. Here he was tried by court-martial and spent the remaining hours of his life writing an apologia for his actions and a long tirade against the men he had helped to mislead. He was hanged on the last day of June from the yardarm of the *Sandwich*. Fifty-eight others were condemned to death, of whom twenty-eight were executed. Others were flogged or sentenced to terms of imprisonment. Of the 412 ringleaders found guilty, 300 were pardoned.

No other end to the affair was possible, for any other would have spelt the loss of naval discipline at a moment when its preservation was vital to the country. When Parker demanded the submission of the Admiralty to a seamen's council and held the nation's trade up to ransom, he threatened to smash the edge of a sharp and delicate instrument which, in Nelson's hand, was about to establish the Pax Britannica and keep free the sea routes of the world for a century. Only undeviating firmness on the part of Admiralty and parliament and an undivided endorsement by the nation could have saved the Navy from the fate of that of Republican France. Mutiny at the Nore had arisen from the same causes as at Spithead and Plymouth. But, with Howe's redress of wellnigh insupportable grievances, naval rebellion in the Thames lost its justification. Its continuance exposed the country to dangers greater than any in her history. In acting as they did, the Government and country showed the soundness of their instincts. So did the seamen in repudiating their leaders.

Yet the mutinies, terrible as they had seemed at the time, had served a purpose. They had brought home to the Government and country the abuses which were impairing the discipline and spirit of the Fleet and which, persisted in, must have proved fatal. Though at first they shook, they helped in the end to restore confidence between ruler and ruled : to re-establish the conditions in which alone officers like Nelson could operate. They began a slow but steady improvement in seagoing conditions : a kind of practical English revolution based not on abstract theories but on concrete needs. Before the Spithead mutiny the men of the Royal Navy, though praised and fêted, were not treated as human beings but as automata : after it their right to decent living and feeding conditions and proper care in sickness, disablement and retirement became gradually recognised. It was something for Englishmen to have initiated such a revolution in time of war and national crisis, and to have done so without disaster.

B

CHAPTER ONE

FIRST BEGINNINGS

At the time of the Spithead and Nore mutinies Horatio Nelson was 38 years old, having been recently awarded the knighthood of the Bath for his part in the defeat of the Spanish fleet off Cape St. Vincent. He was born at Burnham Thorpe in Norfolk on September 27th 1758, the son of a country parson with a large family to support. His mother was a distant kinswoman of the Norfolk squire, Sir Robert Walpole, who had been Britain's first Prime Minister. It was her uncle, Maurice Suckling, captain of a 64-gun battleship, who had given the boy his first chance in life by offering to take him to sea at the age of twelve. 'What has poor little Horatio done that he should be sent to rough it at sea?' he wrote. 'But let him come, and if a cannon ball takes off his head he will at least be provided for.'

Though frail and delicate, the boy's sea training was as varied and thorough as it was rough and harsh. He sailed as a cabin boy in a merchant ship to the West Indies; served, like Drake before him, an apprenticeship in navigation among the shoals of the Thames and Medway and at the age of fourteen, took part in a naval polar expedition, in the course of which he and another boy risked their lives by attempting to capture a bear. By the time he was eighteen he had spent two years as a midshipman on a frigate in the East Indies and, passing the necessary examination for lieutenant, mastered every branch of the seaman's profession. For the next five years he was continuously engaged in the great naval war which followed the American Declaration of Independence when a hard-pressed Britain faced a coalition of all the maritime powers of Europe, eager to take advantage of her foolish quarrel with her colonies. He was still eighteen when he was promoted to his first independent command and by the time the war ended he was, at twenty-two, a post-captain. 'We all rise by deaths,' he wrote to his father. 'I got my rank by a shot killing a post-captain, and I most sincerely hope I shall, when I go, get out of the world the same way.'

This had been his apprenticeship: exercising command in a war when his country was fighting against desperate odds and nothing but the spirit and superlative seamanship and fighting quality of her sailors stood between her and ruin. After the war he served for several years in the West Indies, enforcing the Navigation Laws against the former American colonists, who, having with the help of Britain's enemies won their independence, were no longer as British subjects entitled to carry British goods in their ships. While there he formed a friendship with the king's naval son, Prince William. The future William IV—then a midshipman—wrote of his first meeting with Nelson: 'He appeared the merest boy of a captain I ever beheld. . . . His lank unpowdered hair was tied in a stiff Hessian tail of an extraordinary length; the old-fashioned flaps of his waistcoat added to the general quaintness of his figure. . . . Yet there was something irresistibly pleasing in his address and conversation, and an enthusiasm, when speaking on professional subjects, that showed he was no common being.'

When he was twenty-eight, Nelson met and married a young widow named Mrs. Nisbet, who was living in the island of Nevis. After his ship was paid off at the end of 1787, being unable to support a wife on peacetime service in home waters, he withdrew to Norfolk, where for the next five years he led the life of a poor half-pay officer, eating out his heart ashore, farming his father's glebe and fretting under the tedium of a respectable but, as it turned out, ill-assorted marriage. They were years in which, under its young Prime Minister, William Pitt, a long period of peace for England seemed certain, and disarmament and public retrenchment were the order of the day. Nelson's career seemed finished and he and his friend, the future Admiral Collingwood, then in like retirement, told each other that they despaired of chance ever drawing them back to the seashore.

The unexpected outbreak of the French Revolutionary War in January 1793 found him at the age of thirty-four bombarding the Admiralty with requests for a ship, though it were only a cockle-boat. They gave him a sixty-four-gun ship of the line—a battleship of the second class. For the next four years, despite his frail health, and the loss of his right eye while directing siege operations in Corsica, he was on continuous active service in the Mediterranean. Cheerfully fulfilling every mission entrusted to him, by his enthusiasm to excel in the performance of duty he won a reputation for almost foolhardy gallantry. Leading, as always, by love and example, he filled those who served under him with the same zeal as himself. There was nothing he would not do for his officers and men. There was nothing they would not dare for him.

By the end of 1796, with the conquest of Northern Italy by the brilliant young Revolutionary general, Napoleon Bonaparte, and with the whole of western Europe marshalled against her by France, Britain was forced to recall her Fleet from the Mediterranean in order to defend her own shores. Nelson, now a commodore, was sent by his Commander-in-Chief, Admiral Sir John Jervis, with two frigates to perform the sad mission of evacuating troops and stores from Elba. Off Cartagena, the main Spanish base, he fell in with two enemy frigates and at once engaged them, capturing one. Returning to the Atlantic early in February 1797, his mission accomplished, he found his way barred by a Spanish fleet of twenty-seven battleships and twelve large frigates who were sailing to join the French at Brest with the intention of jointly escorting an army of invasion to Ireland, then on the verge of revolution. Relying on his superior seamanship as they battled with the Atlantic gales, Nelson boldly proceeded to tack his way through them. While his ship was being closely pursued by two battleships, one of his men fell overboard and his First Lieutenant, Hardy, lowered a boat and went to the rescue. To save the man, Nelson, checking the course of his ship, characteristically risked almost certain destruction. But the Spaniards, bewildered by their tiny prey's unaccountable conduct, checked too, and Nelson got away. Next day he rejoined Jervis off Cape St. Vincent, hoisting his Commodore's pennant in the *Captain*, 74.

That night the two fleets drew near. The Spaniards were still ignorant of Jervis's presence, but he, shadowing them with his frigates, was well aware of theirs. The night was misty and the Spanish ships, strung out over many miles of sea, fell into confusion, puncturing the

silence with minute guns. At five o'clock on February
14th—St. Valentine's Day—they were sighted fifteen
miles to the south-west : 'thumpers', as the signal lieutenant of the *Barfleur* reported, 'looming like Beachy Head
in a fog!' Jervis had been reinforced a week before by
five ships from England, but he was still outnumbered
by nearly two to one. Of his fifteen capital ships only
two carried 100 guns, while of the twenty-seven Spanish,
seven were three-deckers with 112 guns or more, one of
them—the four-decker *Santissima Trinidad*—the largest
fighting ship in the world. Yet Jervis was determined to
bar their way and bring them to battle. For a victory at
that moment was essential to his country's safety.

Jervis was no gambler and had reckoned the odds
carefully. He knew the strength of the Spanish fleet but
he also knew its fighting capacity and his own. He
possessed in a supreme degree that comprehensive common sense and balance which, with clarity of decision
and endurance, are the chief attributes of a master of
war. Defeat would spell disaster to England but so
would failure to engage. As the mist lifted and the flag-
lieutenant called out the odds, he remained grimly
unperturbed.

In two columns, imperceptibly merging into an
impenetrable line with sterns and bowsprits almost
touching, the British fleet bore down on the enemy,
making straight for a gap—nearly three miles wide—
between the main force and a straggling division to leeward. It was like the inexorable thrust of a sword into a
lanky giant's careless guard. The Spanish Admiral made
a gallant effort to close it, but too late. The *Principe de
Asturias*—a three-decker of 112 guns—tried to break
through to join the severed squadron only to encounter
the *Victory*'s broadside and drift out of the fight with

tattered sails and splintered topmasts. Then with the *Culloden* leading, Jervis turned into the wind, his ships tacking in turn and meeting the Spanish line on a parallel course. 'Look at Troubridge,' he remarked, with triumph suffusing his stern countenance as the *Culloden* went into action. 'He handles his ship as if the eyes of all England were upon him!'

Down in the dark of the gun decks and in the 'slaughter houses' near the mainmasts, the men waited with the precision born of long practice. As each enemy drew alongside and all was ready—the ports open, matches lighted, the guns run out—they broke into three tremendous cheers more daunting to their foes even than the thunder of their broadsides. 'We gave them their Valentines in style,' wrote one of the gunners of the *Goliath* : 'not that we loved fighting, but we all wished to be free to return to our homes and follow our own pursuits. We knew there was no other way of obtaining this than by defeating the enemy. "The hotter war, the sooner peace," was a saying with us.'

The climax of the battle came at about one o'clock. At that moment the head of the Spanish line was nearing the tail of the British. Nelson, flying his flag in the thirteenth ship in the British line, saw with the instinct of genius that only one thing could prevent the main Spanish division, which had suddenly turned to leeward, from rejoining its isolated ships and so confronting Jervis with a reunited fleet before he could alter course. The Spaniards were battered but they were still intact : another few minutes and the chance of the decisive victory which England needed would have passed.

Without hesitation, disregarding the letter of the orders he had received and anticipating those there was no time to transmit, Nelson bore out of the line and

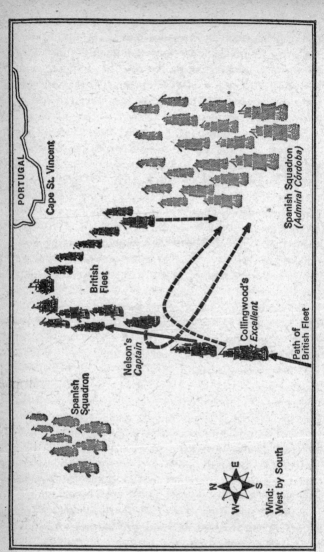

Plan of the Battle of Cape St. Vincent

placed the *Captain*—the smallest two-decker in the British fleet—straight in the course of the giant *Santissima Trinidad* and four other ships. For ten minutes it looked as though the *Captain*, her foremast shot away and her wheelpost broken in a tornado of fire, would be blown out of the water. But when the smoke cleared she was still there, and the *Excellent* under Captain Collingwood was coming to her aid. The Spaniards' line was in inextricable confusion, all hope of a junction between their sundered divisions at an end and Jervis beating back into the fight with the remainder of his fleet.

But before the victory was complete, Nelson did a very remarkable thing. Crippled though she was from her duel with the *Santissima Trinidad*, he placed the *Captain* alongside the 80-gun *San Nicolas* and prepared to board. Helped by a soldier of the 69th, the one-eyed Commodore climbed through the quarter-gallery window in her stern and led his boarders in person through the officers' cabins to the quarterdeck. Here he found Captain Barry, who had jumped into the enemy's mizen chains, already in possession of the poop and hauling down the Spanish Ensign. At that moment fire was opened on the boarding party from the stern-gallery of the three-decker, *San Josef*, which in the confusion of the fight had drifted against the *San Nicolas*. Placing sentries at the tops of the ladders of his still scarcely vanquished prize, Nelson directed his boarding party up the side of the *San Josef*. There, as his friend Collingwood described it, on the quarter-deck of a Spanish first-rate he received the swords of the officers of the two ships, 'while one of his sailors bundled them up with as much composure as he would have made a faggot, though twenty-two of their line were still within gunshot.' Presently the *Victory*, now in the thick of the fight again, passed that triumphant group on the *San Josef*'s quarter-deck, saluting with three cheers. The cool daring of the thing tickled the imagination of the Fleet : 'Nelson's patent bridge for boarding first-rates' became the admiring joke of the lower-deck.

Four battleships, two of them first-rates, remained in the victors' hands. The Spanish fleet, still superior in numbers, withdrew under cover of night to Cadiz, bearing wounds which freed Britain from serious danger in that quarter for many months. The Government, saved at the eleventh hour, showered rewards on the principal commanders. Jervis became Earl St. Vincent with a parliamentary pension of £3,000 a year, the Vice- and Rear-Admirals were made baronets, and another subordinate admiral soon afterwards became an Irish peer. But the hero of the day was the till then unknown Commodore who was created a Knight of the Bath. His sudden exploit had caught England's imagination. For a moment the clouds of that terrible winter parted. Through them men saw the gleam of something swift and glorious and of a new name—Nelson.

CHAPTER TWO

TOUCH AND TAKE

*'I will try to have a motto, or at least it shall
be my watchword—Touch and take!'*

Nelson

The first half of 1797, which saw the victory of Cape St.
Vincent, witnessed also the mutiny of the Channel and
North Sea fleets at Spithead and the Nore. It was a disgrace which never occurred in any ship or squadron in
which Nelson commanded, for everyone who served
under him loved him. That summer Lord St. Vincent—
as Sir John Jervis had now become—sent him with
three ships of the line and four frigates to storm the all
but impregnable Spanish island fortress of Teneriffe
and capture the Mexican treasure fleet which was believed to be sheltering there. On July 20th Nelson
sighted the snow-capped peak and frowning cliffs under
which he was to take his ships. A more desperate enterprise was never attempted. For the all but impregnable
fortress of Santa Cruz bristled with guns and was
defended by eight thousand Spanish troops. Against
them the thirty-eight-year-old Commodore could oppose
a bare thousand sailors and marines. On the night of the
24th, he brought his landing boats to within half a gunshot of the shore before the church bells sounded the
alarm and a hurricane of grapeshot swept the harbour.
With his right arm shattered to the bone, he was borne
half-conscious to his flag-ship. Meanwhile a forlorn hope
of four hundred men under Captain Troubridge carried
the mole and, driving through the deserted streets,

actually reached the great square before their ammunition ran out. Here, from a convent into which they retired, they prepared fireballs and torches to storm their way into the citadel until the Governor—a kindly and sensible man—admiring the extravagance of these mad Englishmen, made propositions so generous that they yielded. Providing them with boats to depart—for their own had been dashed to pieces—he gave each man a loaf of bread and a pint of wine and sent them back to their ships.

Thus in his first independent command as a flag officer Nelson tasted defeat—albeit glorious defeat. He returned to England physically shattered with the hope of ever serving again almost vanished. 'I am become a burden to my friends,' he wrote, 'and useless to my country.'

Yet he was wrong. By the spring of 1798, after nine months painful convalescence, he was able to rejoin his old Commander-in-Chief, Lord St. Vincent, who was still blockading the Spanish fleet off Cadiz. And at that very moment Bonaparte, taking advantage of the continued absence of the British from the Mediterranean, was secretly fitting out a great armada and army to cross that sea, invade Egypt and march on India to make himself master of the eastern world. At that moment, too, the British Government had decided to risk weakening its home defences to send a fleet back to the Mediterranean, not so much with the idea of thwarting Bonaparte's grandiose oriental design—of which it knew nothing—as of rousing Austria and the European Powers to revolt against the French Revolutionary yoke. For knowing that his country could not contend for ever alone against the immense power of France and her continental satellites, the Prime Minister, William

Pitt, was resolved to build up a new coalition against his terrible enemy. It seemed the only way of saving Britain.

Accordingly on May 2nd Cabinet instructions were sent to St. Vincent to detach part of his fleet for a sweep in the Mediterranean. They were accompanied by a private letter from Lord Spencer, the First Lord of the Admiralty. 'When you are apprised,' he wrote, 'that the appearance of a British squadron in the Mediterranean is a condition on which the fate of Europe may at this moment be said to depend, you will not be surprised that we are disposed to strain every nerve and incur considerable hazard in effecting it.' And he went on to suggest that, in the event of St. Vincent not commanding it in person, it should be entrusted to the junior flag officer on the station, Sir Horatio Nelson.

By strange coincidence on the day that this letter was written Nelson had already sailed for the Mediterranean. For within four days of his arrival off Cadiz St. Vincent had ordered him to proceed with three battleships and five small craft to Toulon to report on the preparations and destination of a powerful French fleet. His mission was not to fight but to obtain information. For despite Bonaparte's elaborate attempts at secrecy, rumours of concentrations in Provençal and Italian ports had reached St. Vincent. At Toulon and Marseilles, at Genoa, Civita Vecchia and in Corsica hundreds of transports were assembling, troops embarking, and battleships, frigates and corvettes moving into position for some great venture.

Thus, nearing his fortieth year, Nelson now a Rear-Admiral, was again in independent command, with his reputation after his setback at Teneriffe, a little uncertain, as of a man too reckless for his age. His countrymen, slow to recognise intellect, knew his courage and ardour but had little conception of the quality of his mind. They had yet to realise its infinite capacity for taking pains, its knife-like penetration, its brilliant clarity. Its very lucidity, reducing every scheme and command to elemental terms such as a child could understand, tended to deceive them. They thought of him as a simple sailorman. They never conceived of him, till his miraculous deeds enlightened them, as the supreme embodiment of the genius of their country.

After many years of apprenticeship, he was now to be pitted against Napoleon, the most dazzling genius of his age—himself the embodiment of that great and terrifying explosion of human energy, the Revolution which England was struggling to hold in bounds. Nelson's success or failure was to depend on his ability to guess and anticipate the thoughts of his brilliant adversary. To that test he brought qualities of an almost unique order : immense professional knowledge and experience, the fruits of life-long application and discipline, selfless devotion to duty, inspired courage, a great heart and the imagination which can mobilise the evidence of the present and past to predict the future. His was that strange combination of brooding patience, study and intense concentration with a mercurial temperament which rose like lightning out of storm and in the hour chosen of destiny lighted the path to victory. Above all his power was based, like his country's, on adherence to moral law : once he was convinced that a course was right, nothing could shake his constancy to it and the burning tenacity of his purpose. The strength of his will was equal to Napoleon's. And because it derived more consistently from enduring principles it prevailed.

Nelson's career of fame rose from victory to ever greater victory. Napoleon's rose and then fell.

On May 8th 1798, Nelson left Gibraltar with three ships of the line and five frigates, sailing at dusk to conceal his eastward course from watching eyes. Nine days later, cruising in the Gulf of Lyons, one of his frigates captured a French corvette from Toulon whose crew under examination disclosed that the famous General Bonaparte had arrived in the port from Paris, that thousands of troops were embarking and that fifteen battleships of the line were waiting to sail.

Had it not been for the usual confusion and corruption of the Revolutionary ports they would have sailed already. Nearly 40,000 picked troops, more than three hundred transports and fifty warships had been assembled. This huge armada was laden not only with horse, foot, artillery and stores of war but with engineers, architects and professors of every science and art, 'from astronomers down to washerwomen'. It was equipped for colonisation as well as for conquest and commanded by a brilliant galaxy of talent.

On the 19th the main division of the expedition, with Bonaparte himself aboard, weighed from Toulon, coasting north-eastwards along the Riviera in the direction of Genoa to gather its consorts. Nelson did not see it sail for he was still some way from the port. On the following night his flagship, the *Vanguard*, suffered an unexpected disaster, her newly-commissioned crew losing main and mizen topmasts and foremast in a sudden gale. For two days she was battered by the waves off the Sardinian coast and was only saved from total wreck by the cool daring of Captain Ball of the *Alexander*, who took her in tow and persisted, in spite of intense danger to his own ship, in bringing her under the lee of San Pietro Island.

Here, on May 24th, Nelson wrote to his wife to tell her of the setback. 'I firmly believe that it was the Almighty's goodness to check my consummate vanity.' In four days of Herculean labour, the *Vanguard* was rigged with jury-masts and made fit for sea. Then with his three battleships Nelson sailed for the secret rendezvous where his frigates, scattered by the storm, were to have awaited him. But when he reached it on June 4th the frigates were not there. Next day, still waiting, he received momentous tidings. For Hardy in the dispatch brig *Mutine* arriving from Cadiz brought news not only of the errant frigates which, despairing of the *Vanguard*'s plight, had gone to Gibraltar, but of Nelson's appointment to the command of a fleet. The opportunity for which he had waited so long had arrived.

It had come at a strange and critical moment. Bonaparte had sailed a fortnight before and had gone no one knew where. A few days after Nelson had left Cadiz, St. Vincent had received Spencer's instructions about sending a fleet into the Mediterranean. Though the Spaniards, under orders from Paris, made as if about to put out to sea, the old admiral never hesitated. On May 19th he despatched Hardy with Nelson's commission. On the 21st, without even waiting for the arrival of the promised reinforcements from England, he sent Troubridge with his ten finest battleships and captains—the elite of the fleet—to join Nelson.

On June 6th Troubridge found his new commander. It was characteristic of Nelson that he refused to transfer his flag from the storm-battered *Vanguard*. His two other battleships were beyond the horizon searching for the newcomers. He did not wait for them but left the fifty-gun *Leander* to bid them to follow. His orders were couched in the broadest terms. He was to pursue the Toulon fleet and attack it wherever found. Since Britain had no base in the Mediterranean, and necessity dictated, he was not to stand on ceremony with neutrals. Should they out of terror of the French refuse to grant him supplies, he was to compel them at the cannon's mouth.

His instructions gave him little clue as to Bonaparte's destination. They mentioned Naples, Sicily, Portugal and Ireland—now in open rebellion—but made no reference to Egypt. He had no reliable information as to the strength of the French fleet, though he believed it to consist of fifteen or sixteen ships of the line. He knew even less of its whereabouts. Having no frigates he could not comb the seas for intelligence. He had only the light of his intellect to follow and the strength of his will. 'Be they bound to the Antipodes,' he assured Spencer, 'your Lordship may rely that I will not lose a moment in bringing them to action.'

Following the course of the French Nelson skirted the Genoese Riviera and Italian coast. The seas were strangely empty, for the French control of the Mediterranean had banished most of its former commerce. Day after day no sail appeared on the blue horizon. Once a convoy of distant Spanish merchantmen was sighted— plunder that might have made Nelson and his captains rich with prize money and bought him some fine estate in England with white Jane Austen house and trim lawns and deer park. But his mind was set on his purpose and he let them pass unmolested. He dared not lose an hour.

On June 14th, while far away the fate of Ireland

trembled in the balance and the rebel leaders in the green-bannered camp on Vinegar Hill waited for the tidings of French sails, Nelson obtained second-hand news from a passing ship that ten days earlier a great fleet had been seen to the west of Sicily. He accordingly sent the *Mutine* ahead to Naples with a letter begging Sir William Hamilton, the British Ambassador, to urge the King of the Two Sicilies and his English-born Prime Minister, Acton, to shake off their subservience to the dreaded Jacobins and strike while the iron was hot. On the 17th he arrived off the port to learn what he had already suspected : that the French had gone to Malta and were either about to attack or had already attacked that island stronghold.

In a fever of excitement he wrote again to Hamilton. The Neapolitan king, who hated the French, whose sister-in-law Marie Antoinette, had died on the scaffold in Paris, and who had secretly implored British aid, had a unique opportunity to strike a blow which could save his throne, liberate Italy and shatter the dark clouds that hung over Europe. The most formidable of French generals and the flower of the French Army were at his mercy. For though Nelson had with him a matchless instrument, it could only do the work of a fleet. To destroy the enemy if at Malta, he needed fireships, gun-boats and bomb vessels; to annihilate their transports if at sea, he must have frigates. The court of the Two Sicilies, if it would take its courage in its hands, could supply both. 'The King of Naples,' he wrote, 'may now have part of the glory in destroying these pests of the human race; and the opportunity, once lost, may never be regained.'

Yet though the timorous Italians sent good wishes and a secret promise of supplies, they would dare no more.

Nelson must beat the French before they would stir, even though their inertness should rob him of all chance of victory and themselves of survival. Without wasting time, though still bombarding Hamilton with letters, he pressed through the Straits of Messina and, crowding on all sail, hurried southward down the coast of Sicily heading for Malta where he hoped to catch the enemy at anchor. On the 22nd at the southern point of Sicily off Cape Passaro the *Mutine* fell in with a Genoese brig and learnt from her master that the French had already captured Malta from the Knights of St. John—which was true—and, which was not true, had sailed again on the 16th eastward bound.

With the instinct of genius, though his instructions had given him no inkling of it, Nelson had already divined Bonaparte's intention. A few days earlier he had written to Spencer, 'If they pass Sicily, I shall believe they are going on their scheme of possessing Alexandria and getting troops to India.' He had been strictly cautioned against allowing the French to get to the west of him lest they should slip through the Straits of Gibraltar. But he reckoned that with the prevailing westerly winds Bonaparte's vast and unwieldy armada had little chance of beating back to the Atlantic. Egypt on the other hand would be an easy run for it. If Bonaparte had left Malta on the 16th, he must already be nearly at Alexandria.

Nelson, therefore, decided to act. He called a council of his captains, but the result was a foregone conclusion. Men like himself in the prime of life—their average age was under forty—they were little given to hesitation. They endorsed his opinion that all the probabilities—the seizure of Malta, the reported equipment of the expedition, the direction of the wind and the enemy's point of

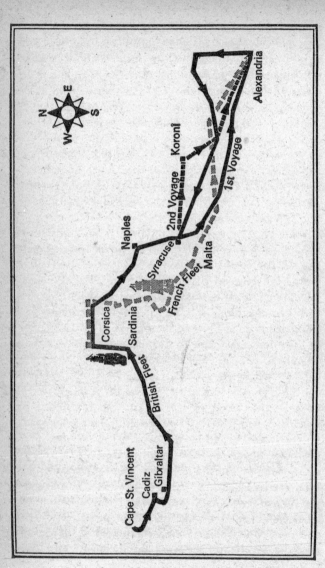

Nelson's chase of the French fleet around the Mediterranean, 1798

sailing—pointed to Bonaparte's having gone to Egypt. The safe course would be for the British to await events where they were : guarding the two Sicilies, keeping the weather gauge and making sure that the enemy could not get to westward and threaten England and her blockading squadrons in the Atlantic. A lesser man than Nelson, playing for his professional career and safety from official censure, would have taken it. Yet to have done so would have been to abandon that for which he had set out : the annihilation of the French fleet and transports. With the stake nothing less than the future of the world, he at once set course for Alexandria.

•   •   •

But the French had not sailed from Malta on June 16th. They had appeared off the island on the 9th and summoned its international and age-long custodians, the Knights of St. John, to surrender. The scene had been carefully set. The Maltese had no stomach for their rich and obese masters' cause, the island was swarming with French agents and traitors, and the Knights, comfortably set in their ways and undermined by subtle propaganda, were divided as to the advisability of resistance. After three days discussion they surrendered, and Bonaparte, whose besieging armada would otherwise have fallen an easy prey for Nelson on the 22nd, took possession of Valetta—'the strongest place in Europe'. Here he remained for nearly a week, helping himself to the accumulations of seven centuries of luxurious and cultured living. Then, leaving a strong garrison behind him to hold the strategic half-way house to France, he sailed on the 19th for Alexandria.

So it came about that Nelson's look-outs on June 22nd saw the sails of French frigates on the far horizon.

But he did not stop to investigate them for he supposed
that they could not belong to Bonaparte's main fleet
which, according to his information, had left Malta six
days before. Had he possessed any frigates of his own,
he would soon have discovered his error. But to have
pursued the French frigates with his battle fleet would
have led him nowhere, for they would inevitably have
lured him away from his real quarry, the great ships and
transports. So instead he kept on his course. Shortly
afterwards darkness fell, and during the night, which
was hazy, the British line of battle, swift, compact and
intent, passed unknowing through the converging track
of the French expedition. The sound of the British
minute guns firing through the mist caused the French
admiral to sheer away to the northward in the direction of Crete. Had dawn come half an hour earlier it
would have revealed him and his helpless transports.
But by sunrise on the 23rd the last French sails were
just below the horizon.

That was one of the decisive moments of the world's
history. A long train of events had brought the two
fleets to that place at that hour, of which the most
important were Bonaparte's dynamic ambition and
Nelson's zeal for duty. Had they clashed the result
would have been certain : the elite and cadre of the
Grande Armée would have found a watery grave seventeen years before Waterloo, and its terrible chieftain
would either have shared it or become a prisoner of the
English. For superior though they were in size and gun-
power on paper, the French battleships would have been
no match on the open sea for the British. Old and shame-
fully neglected during their long-enforced sojourn in
port, destitute of marine stores and crowded with
soldiers, they could never have withstood those lean,

stripped, storm-tested dogs of war from St. Vincent's fleet. Their crews, drawn from the lawless dregs of the Revolutionary ports, had had little training in gunnery or manoeuvre. Nelson knew exactly what to do. Thanks to the Cabinet's bold resolution, to St. Vincent's discipline, above all to his own inspired fixity of purpose, the blundering, persistent patience of Pitt's England seemed on the afternoon of June 22nd 1798, about to be rewarded. Bonaparte, epitomising the Revolutionary weakness for desperate gambling, had staked everything on Britain's not being able to send a fleet to the Mediterranean. And now at the moment that he was reaching out to grasp the prize of the Orient, the British fleet crossed his path.

Crossed it and vanished. The Corsican's star had proved too strong and bright for the clumsy purpose of England. But Bonaparte's fortune did not lie only in his star. With all his genius, he could not understand why his admirals trembled so at the thought of encountering a British fleet in mid-ocean. He had forty thousand soldiers with him : he had only to close and let them board the English corsairs. He had never seen the destructive power of a British man-of-war in action : could not, battle-scarred though he was, conceive it. Not destiny—which had still to obliterate his bright name— but an error of Britain's had saved him. Lack of frigates alone robbed Nelson of a victory that would have been Trafalgar and Waterloo in one. Again and again St. Vincent had pleaded with the Admiralty for more frigates : pleaded in vain. He had had to send his brilliant subordinate into the Mediterranean with too few, and these—now vainly seeking him—had failed him. Treasury parsimony, the unpreparedness of a peace-loving people, above all the needs of restless, ill-treated

Ireland had all contributed to this fatal flaw. It was to
cost Britain and the civilised world seventeen more years
of war, waste and destruction.

.   .   .

So it came about that on June 23rd 1798 the two fleets,
having converged, passed out of reach of one another,
Brueys with his momentous freight edging cumbrously
northwards towards the greater security of Crete, Nelson
with every inch of canvas spread direct for Alexandria
hoping to catch Bonaparte before he could disembark.
'We are proceeding,' wrote Captain Saumarez of the
Orion, 'upon the merest conjecture only, and not on any
positive information. Some days must now elapse before
we can be relieved from our cruel suspense.' On the
sixth day Nelson reached Alexandria and to his un-
speakable chagrin found the roads empty. No one had
seen anything of Bonaparte's armada, though the sleepy
Turkish authorities were making languid preparations to
repel it and threatening to decapitate any belligerent
who dared to land in their country. Still believing in his
false information that the French had left Malta on the
16th, it never occurred to Nelson that they had not yet
covered the distance. Without waiting he at once put to
sea again, steering for the Syrian coast in hope of news
of a landing at Aleppo or an attack on the Dardanelles.

As, early on June 29th, the British sails dropped over
the eastern horizon, watchers at Alexandria saw those of
the French rise over the western. Hampered by its lack
of skill, vast size and triangular course, Bonaparte's
expedition, averaging only fifty miles a day, had taken
just double the time of its pursuer to reach Egypt. Once
more, cruelly crippled by lack of frigates, Nelson had

missed an epoch-making victory by a few hours. With nearly four hundred vessels the French had crossed the Mediterranean and had not lost a ship. With the superb arrogance of their race and revolutionary creed they boasted that the British had not dared to measure their strength against them.

Though he had still no idea how narrow had been his escape, Bonaparte wasted no time before disembarking. On July 1st he landed : on the 5th he stormed Alexandria, putting all who resisted to the sword. A fortnight later, advancing at his habitual speed across the desert, he routed the main Egyptian army under the shadow of the Pyramids. On the 22nd he entered Cairo. Another nation had been overwhelmed.

Meanwhile Nelson, fretting with impatience and full of remorse for the kingdom of the Two Sicilies, had sought in vain for his elusive quarry in the Gulf of Alexandretta. Thence, skirting the shores of Crete, he beat back against westerly winds to Syracuse. Years later he told Troubridge that in his mortification he believed he had almost died through swelling of the vessels of the heart. To St. Vincent, to whom he wrote to ease his mind, he declared that the only valid objection he could conceive against the course he had taken was that he should not have gone such a long voyage without more certain information. 'My answer is ready—"Who was I to get it from?" Was I to wait patiently till I heard certain accounts? If Egypt was their object, before I could hear of them they would have been in India. To do nothing, I felt, was disgraceful : therefore I made use of my understanding and by it I ought to stand or fall. I am before your Lordship's judgement (which in the present case I feel is the tribunal of my country) and, if under all the circumstances it is decided that I am wrong, I ought, for the sake of the country, to be superseded.'

Already in England men who knew nothing of the circumstances were saying that he should be. The news of his appointment had been greeted with a clamour of tongues. Collingwood wrote from Cadiz that the resignation of two senior admirals, furious at being passed over, had interrupted all intercourse of friendship in St. Vincent's fleet, which was in consequence in a most unpleasant state. Their friends and many others now said that Nelson had blundered and that a man not yet forty was not fit to command a fleet on so important a service. Tempers were short in England in the summer of 1798: the long suspense of the previous year, the naval mutinies at Spithead and the Nore and the reaction when no invasion came were beginning to fray men's nerves. The Irish rebellion, suppressed after four anxious weeks, was still simmering. It was known that Bonaparte was at large and that his pursuer had failed to find him. He might by now be in Naples or he might be sailing towards Ireland. All that was certain was that Nelson had missed him, had bungled his mission. There were demands for his recall and for the resignation of the Ministers who had appointed him.

On July 19th, with his water nearly exhausted, Nelson reached Syracuse, having in his own words gone a round of six hundred leagues with an expedition incredible and being at the end of it as ignorant of the enemy's situation as at the beginning. 'The Devil's children,' he wrote, 'have the Devil's luck!' His only thought was to be off again. He suffered agonies when the governor of the port, standing on his neutrality, refused to admit more than four ships at a time for revictualling. 'Our treatment is scandalous for a great nation to put up with,' he wrote to Lady Hamilton, 'and the king's flag is insulted. . . . If we are to be kicked in every port of the Sicilian dominions, the sooner we are gone the better. . . . I have only to pray I may find the French and throw all my vengeance on them.'

But when the tactful offices of the Hamiltons at the Neapolitan Court had secured an open welcome and ample supplies for the fleet, the essential magnanimity of the man returned. He reproached nobody but himself. 'Your Lordship,' he wrote to St. Vincent, 'deprived yourself of frigates to make mine the first squadron in the world. . . . But if the French are above water, I will find them out and if possible bring them to battle. You have done your part in giving me so fine a fleet, and I hope to do mine in making use of them.'

On July 25th he was ready once more for sea. Disregarding the protests of the Neapolitan Prime Minister, who wished him to stand sentinel over the Two Sicilies, he sailed again, this time—since all intelligence showed that the French were not to the west of him—towards the Morea. With all canvas spread the great ships sped on their search—*Culloden, Theseus, Alexander,* and *Swiftsure; Vanguard, Minotaur, Defence, Audacious, Zealous, Orion, Goliath, Majestic, Bellerophon.* The sea was empty, for their journeying had filled the French authorities in every port of southern Europe with dread and no merchantman dared put to sea. They sailed in order of battle, in three compact divisions in case the enemy should be encountered at sea : two to tackle Brueys' battle fleet and the other to do the work of the missing frigates and destroy the transports.

Every day throughout the long chase the men were exercised at their guns and small arms. Whenever the weather permitted the captains went aboard the

Vanguard to discuss with the admiral the precise function which each was to fulfil in battle. In the 'school for captains' on Nelson's quarterdeck they unconsciously entered into his mind till each of his ideas—lucid, precise and devised against every eventuality—became as natural to them as to him. Long linked by the comradeship of sea and service, these rough, weather-beaten men, with their wonderful professional skill, were distilled into a single instinctive instrument of war in the alembic of Nelson's mind and spirit. They became what in his love he called them—a band of brothers.

The keynote of the fleet's readiness for battle was a minute imaginative attention to detail : the sure hallmark of a great leader. 'No man,' Mahan has written, 'was ever better served than Nelson by the inspiration of the hour; no man ever counted less on it.' Every ship was ready day and night for action : every man schooled in an exact part. Five thousand wills and bodies moved to a single purpose infinitely diversified in individual function. It was a living discipline which wasted nothing; of muscle, mind or matter. Everything was prepared because everything was foreseen. Thus in the *Alexander* Captain Ball had every spare shroud and sail constantly soaked in water and rolled tight into hard non-inflammable cylinders.

On July 28th, three days after leaving Syracuse, Nelson obtained news of the French from some Greek fishermen in the Gulf of Koron. A month before, a great fleet had been seen spread far over the seas sailing southeastwards from Crete. With the wind in the west for the past month it was evidence enough. Bonaparte must have gone to Egypt after all. Once more all sail was set for Alexandria.

A little before noon on August 1st 1798, the Pharos of

Alexandria became visible and soon after the minarets
of the city and the masts of merchantmen in the port.
But of the French fleet there was no sign. Sending the
Swiftsure and *Alexander* in to investigate more closely,
Nelson sadly turned eastwards along the coast as he had
done a month before. Dinner was a meal of gloom on
every ship: 'I do not recollect,' wrote Captain
Saumarez of the *Orion*, 'ever to have felt so utterly
hopeless as when we sat down. Judge what a change
took place when, as the cloth was being removed, the
officer of the watch came running in saying, "Sir, a
signal is just now made that the enemy is in Aboukir
Bay and moored in a line of battle!"' In an instant
every one was on his feet and every glass charged. As
Saumarez came out of his cabin on to the quarterdeck,
the crew broke into exultant cheers.

At the masthead of the *Goliath*, leading the fleet with
the *Zealous*, the straining eyes of Midshipman Elliot,
scanning the low Egyptian shore in the hot haze, had
caught the first sight of those heavenly masts. Fearing to
hail the quarterdeck, lest keen ears in the *Zealous*
should hear and gain the credit, the exultant boy slid
quickly down a backstay and ran to Captain Foley with
his tidings. But before the fluttering signal 'Enemy in
sight', could reach the masthead, *Zealous* had guessed
the meaning of the scurry and cluster of flags on the
deck of her sister ship and had been before her. As the
signal reached each crowded ship, a 'wave of joy' ran
through the fleet. Nelson, whose inflexible will had
equalled Bonaparte's, had run his quarry to earth at
last. 'If we succeed,' cried Berry voicing his unspoken
thought, 'what will the world say?' 'There is no *if* in
the case,' replied Nelson, 'that we shall succeed is certain;
who will live to tell the story is a very different question.'

Fifteen miles east of Alexandria the French battle fleet lay at anchor in a great bay guarded by shoals to eastward and by the batteries of Aboukir Castle at its western end. There were sixteen ships in all, thirteen of the line with the *Orient*, Admiral Brueys' giant flagship, in the centre of the line. They lay as close inshore as the sandbanks allowed, forming for nearly two miles a line of thousands of guns with 160 yards between each ship. At the head of the line, guarding it from approach from the west, lay Aboukir island crowned with mortars.

At half-past two, about the same time as the pursuers sighted their prey, the French look-outs saw the British sails. As his van was so strongly protected and as to attack his centre or rear his assailants would have to face the concentrated fire of his whole line, Brueys felt convinced that there would be no battle that day. It was to his advantage that it should be postponed. His ships were bigger than the British and more heavily gunned, but many of his men were ashore, discipline was lax and the decks were cumbered with stores and booty. Only the most reckless of foes would be likely to attack him in so strong a position with equal or inferior force. By the time they could reach the bay and negotiate the sandbanks it would be almost dark. It would be insanity for them to attack at night. Brueys, like most ordinary commanders, was a static man and he imagined that he had to do with static men like himself.

But the British squadron never paused. It came on out of the west with all sails set. For Nelson at his journey's end was as eager to do that for which he had come as Bonaparte had been to land and take possession of Egypt. His sufferings and anxiety were over at last. He viewed the obstacles, his flag-captain noted, with the eye of a seaman determined on attack. He saw the strength of the French centre, where Brueys had concentrated his greatest ships and of its rear where the next strongest were gathered. But he also saw the weakness of the van if he could bring his fleet round inside the island and pass between it and the leading ships. And though he had no chart of the shoals except a rough plan taken from a prize, 'it instantly struck his eager and penetrating mind that where there was room for an enemy's ship to swing, there was room for one of his to anchor.'

It had always been Nelson's plan, discussed on innumerable occasions with his captains, should he find the enemy at anchor to throw the whole weight of his strength on a part of their line and crush it before the rest could come to its aid. Only by doing so could he win the annihilating victory which it was his purpose to achieve. The ding-dong battles of the past two centuries, in which every Englishman laid himself alongside a Frenchman and battered away till one side tired and drew off, could not give it him. There was only just time to work round the island and the shoals before night fell; three of his thirteen capital ships—the *Swiftsure* and *Alexander* reconnoitring Alexandria, and the *Culloden* towing a prize—were some miles away and could not reach the scene of battle before darkness.

There was no opportunity for consultation or elaborate signals, but there was no need for them. Every captain knew what was in his admiral's mind. At five-thirty he flew the signal to form line of battle in order of sailing, and silently and imperceptibly without slackening their majestic advance the great ships slid into their appointed places. The *Goliath*, whose look-out midshipman had revenged himself on his rival in the *Zealous* by anticipating Nelson's signal while it was still fluttering to

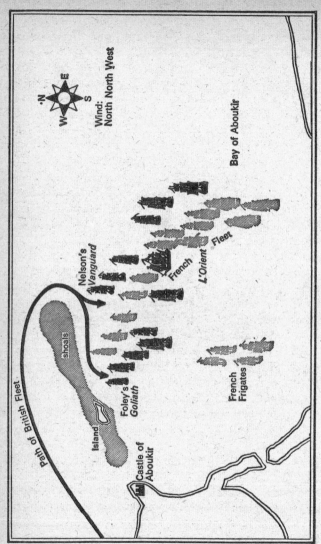

Plan of the Battle of the Nile

Nelson at twenty-three

A specially composed picture of Nelson's flagships,
H.M.S. *Victory* is on the right

'Jack in the Bilboes': a forceful method of the press gang

A contemporary illustration of the scene on the main deck of a
battleship in harbour in the early nineteenth century

the masthead, took the lead. The flagship dropped back
to the sixth place where the Admiral could exercise control of the battle, seeing how his leading ships fared and
using his position to vary the disposition of the remaining five.

In the hour of suspense Nelson gave two other orders.
In order to guide the latecomers and avoid the danger
of Briton firing on Briton, every ship was directed to
hoist four lights at the mizen peak. And on reaching her
allotted station she was to anchor by the stern instead of
by the head and so place herself in immediate fighting
posture. By this simple precaution the enemy was denied
the opportunity of raking each British ship as her bows
swung round into the wind.

Having rounded the island and 'hauled well round all
dangers', the ships, avoiding the direct approach, short-
ened sail and hugging the coast worked their way to
windward of the van—the weakest, because in his belief
the securest, part of Brueys' position. The sun was just
setting—'and a red and fiery sun it was'—as they went
into the bay. Down below the men were stripping to
their trousers, opening the ports and clearing for action.

It had been Nelson's plan to anchor one of his ships
alternately on the bow and quarter of each of the leading Frenchmen. But whether by an eleventh hour sug-
gestion of the admiral or by his own inspiration Captain
Foley of the *Goliath*, who was the only officer in the
fleet with a French chart, rounded the head of the
enemy lines and, sounding as he went through the shallow waters, attacked it from the shoreward side. It was
a feat of superb seamanship. Relying on the proximity
of the sandbanks the French had never conceived such a
thing possible and, feeling themselves safe, had not even
taken the trouble to clear the port batteries, which were

C

carelessly cluttered up with stores. *Zealous, Orion, Theseus* and *Audacious* followed *Goliath*. As each leviathan swept past the undefended flank of the leading French ships she swept them in turn with a fire that left them helpless and broken. Within ten minutes all the *Guerrier*'s masts were gone, and within ten minutes more the *Conquerant*'s and *Spartiate*'s.

Meanwhile Nelson led the *Vanguard* and the remaining ships against the other side of the French line. By seven o'clock, within half an hour of the commencement of the action, the five leading French seventy-fours were being raked by eight ships of similar size and greatly superior to them in gunnery while their consorts to leeward watched helpless and inactive. Two British ships, the *Majestic* and *Bellerophon*, over-shooting their mark in the growing darkness, engaged the French centre, the first losing her captain in a swift interchange of broadsides with the *Heureuse*, and then passing on to engage the *Mercure*, while the second audaciously placed herself alongside Brueys' flagship, *Orient*—a vessel nearly twice her size.

Wrought to the highest tension by their long, tenacious pursuit, the British fought, as Berry put it, with an ardour and vigour impossible to describe. The French also fought with great gallantry. But the British were fighting with the certain conviction of victory and, every man knowing what to do in all emergencies, with an order and freedom from confusion absent in the Republican ships. Early in the engagement, when the issue was already a foregone conclusion, Nelson was struck on the forehead by a piece of flying iron from the *Spartiate*. Flung to the deck and blinded by the strip of bleeding flesh that fell over his solitary eye, he was carried below thinking himself a dying man. Here in the crowded cockpit he lay in intense pain, insisting on taking his turn at the surgeon with the other wounded men and constantly calling with what he believed to be his dying breath for news of the battle. Once he bade Berry hail the *Minotaur*, anchored ahead of the *Vanguard*, that he might thank Captain Louis for his conduct before he died. Already three enemy ships had struck and three more were disabled, and with his brain wandering a little he endeavoured to dictate a dispatch to the Admiralty. His secretary was too overwrought to write, so the blinded man took the pen himself and with trembling hand traced the words: 'Almighty God has blessed His Majesty's arms . . .'.

By now the British reserve was entering the fight. The *Culloden*, the finest ship in the fleet, had met with disaster, her brave Captain Troubridge in his anxiety to arrive in time, having taken the island too close and struck on the tail of the shoal. Here he remained all night in full view of the battle and in a state of agitation impossible to conceive, suffering the pounding of the sea and struggling to clear his vessel. But he served as a beacon for the *Swiftsure* and *Alexander* hurrying up from the west. The two great ships, furiously fired at by the battery on the island, rounded the reef safely in the haze and darkness and swept down on the centre of the French line, guided by the flashes of the guns and the lanterns gleaming through the British gun ports. In both vessels absolute silence was preserved, no sound being heard but the helmsman's orders and the shout of the leadsman calling the depths.

At one moment a dark shape loomed up in front of the *Swiftsure*. It was the *Bellerophon*, dismasted after her duel with the *Orient*, drifting out of the fight with a third of her crew dead or disabled. Only Captain Hallowell's flawless discipline prevented her from being swept by the *Swiftsure*'s guns before her identity was revealed. But, despite the suspense and the spasmodic fire of the French, not a shot was fired. At 8.3 p.m. precisely the *Swiftsure* dropped into the *Bellerophon*'s vacant berth two hundred yards from the French flagship. At 8.5, anchored and with her sails clewed up, she opened up with a tremendous broadside. A few minutes later Captain Ball in the *Alexander* followed suit.

It was about nine o'clock when Hallowell, still fresh to the fight, noticed flames pouring out of one of the cabins of the *Orient*. He at once directed every available gun on the spot. The fire spread quickly because of the oil, paint and other combustibles which had been left about the French flagship. As the great vessel, the finest in the Republican Navy, blazed more fiercely, every British ship in the neighbourhood trained her guns on her. Down in the hold of his flagship Nelson heard of the impending fatality and insisted on being led up on deck to watch; as soon as he saw her imminence of doom he ordered the *Vanguard*'s only undamaged boat to be lowered to rescue the survivors. With the fire racing downwards towards the *Orient*'s magazine, the ships about her closed their hatches or drifted away to avoid the explosion. Only *Swiftsure* and *Alexander* remained firing grimly up to the last moment, with long lines of men with buckets stationed to extinguish the outburst when it came.

At a quarter to ten the *Orient* blew up with a terrifying detonation. The shocks could be felt by French watchers at Rosetta ten miles away; down in the magazine of the *Goliath* the boys and women at their blind, monotonous task of passing up the powder thought that the after-part of their own vessel had exploded. The whole bay was lit as brightly as day by the expiring flame of the great ship as she rose in the air. After she vanished, silence fell on the combatants : then after some minutes the guns opened out again. As they did so the moon rose dazzling in her Egyptian beauty over the wreckage and slaughter.

Yet though the night was still young the battle was losing momentum. With the great admiral who had conceived it dazed and disabled by his wound, the soul was gone out of it. Five of the French ships had already struck : another, the 80-gun *Franklin*, was failing fast. But the victors after sailing and fighting all day were exhausted. They would fire for a time and then desist : all night the battle flared up and then died away. 'My people was so extremely jaded,' reported Captain Miller of the *Theseus*, 'that as soon as they had hove our sheet anchor up they dropped under the capstan bars and were asleep in a moment in every sort of posture.' After the surrender of the *Franklin* the second lieutenant of *Alexander* approached Ball to tell him that, though the hearts of his men were as good as ever, they could do no more and begged him to let them sleep for half an hour by their guns. Nelson's slightly disjointed messages speeding through the night were received rather than obeyed : in that confused interminable nightmare of weariness nothing was ever quite carried through to an end.

As it began to grow light the magnitude of the victory became apparent. At 5.27 a.m. Captain Hallowell noted that six enemy battleships had struck their colours; on board his own ship 'carpenters were busy stopping the shot holes, . . . people employed knotting and splicing the rigging.' At six he heard the minute guns of the *Majestic* firing as she buried her captain.

The whole bay was floating with charred wreckage and
dead bodies, mangled and scorched. By this time it was
light enough to see that three other battleships were at
the victors' mercy : dismasted hulks aground or drifting.
Only Villeneuve's three spectators in the rear remained
uninjured. Presently these slipped their anchors and began to bear out to sea. But one of them, the *Timoleon*,
in her haste to be gone ran on to the sandbanks. Her
crew swam ashore and made off inland, a cloud of
smoke revealing that her captain had fired her. Alone of
the thirteen French ships of the line the *Guillaume Tell*,
and the *Généreux* with two frigates, escaped into the
blue of the Mediterranean. For a while *Theseus*, the
only British ship sufficiently undamaged to carry sail,
pursued them till a signal from the Admiral recalled
her.

In the first aftermath of battle Nelson and his men
could scarcely conceive the fullness of what they had
done. All day on August 2nd they were engaged in
fishing naked prisoners from rafts and floating wreckage. More than two thousand unwounded prisoners were
taken and nearly fifteen hundred wounded : that night
Nelson dined half a dozen wounded French captains in
his cabin. Brueys, the first admiral in France, had been
cut in half by a cannon ball before the *Orient* blew up.
Two thousand more of his men had been killed or
drowned, nine of his thirteen battleships captured, two
more destroyed. Nothing like it had been known since
the day when the Duke of Marlborough had entertained
a French Marshal and two generals in his coach after
Blenheim.

For it was not so much defeat that the French had
suffered as annihilation. Though superior to their
assailants by thirty per cent in men and twenty per cent

in weight of broadside, and fighting in a chosen position in a dangerous bay with the head of their line protected by shore batteries, they had been overwhelmed by the skill and ferocity of the attack. In a few hours they had literally been blown out of the water. And the price paid by the victors had been scarcely two hundred men killed and seven hundred wounded. It was an astonishing testimony to the intensity and accuracy of British gunfire, to Nelson's leadership and to the new school of close fighting he had initiated. Above all it revealed, in the hands of an inspired commander, the quality of British discipline. In his general order thanking his men Nelson, recalling the mutinies of the previous summer, emphasised this point. 'It must strike forcibly every British seaman how superior their conduct is, when in discipline and good order, to the riotous behaviour of lawless Frenchmen.' Nothing so deeply impressed the same lawless Frenchmen, many of them professed atheists, as the religious service which was held on the morrow of the battle on the splintered, bloodstained decks of the British flagship. It struck them as an extraordinary thing that six hundred men—the roughest of the rough—could be assembled for such a purpose amid the scene of so much carnage and profess their mild faith with such order and quietness.

* * *

Because of Nelson's lack of frigates and the very depth of his penetration into the French position, the news of his achievement travelled slowly. Its effect was not an instantaneous explosion but the spluttering of a charge of powder. For many days after the battle the victors remained in Egyptian waters, remote from a world that had lost trace of them. It took Nelson a fortnight before

he could make his dismasted prizes fit for sea. Three he
was forced to burn : the other six he sent off to Gibraltar on August 14th under escort of seven of his battleships. Their progress up the Mediterranean was painfully
slow.

Want of frigates, Nelson wrote, would be found
stamped on his heart. The first vessel available to carry
the report of the victory to St. Vincent, the 50-gun
Leander, did not leave Aboukir Bay until nearly a week
after the battle. As ill-luck would have it, she and Captain Berry—the bearer of the official dispatches—were
captured twelve days later in a calm by one of the two
fugitive survivors of Brueys' line of battle.

So it came about that no intelligence of the victory
reached western Europe till September 4th, when it was
brought to Naples by the *Mutine* sloop, which Nelson,
on the arrival of his long-lost frigates, had sent off with
duplicate dispatches on August 14th. Before they
arrived Nelson himself was on his way to Europe. On
August 14th he had received a summons from St.
Vincent to return to save the kingdom of the Two
Sicilies from the threat of seaborne invasion and co-
operate in the capture of a British Mediterranean base
in the Balearics. Accordingly, leaving three battleships
and three frigates under Captain Hood to blockade
Egypt, Nelson reluctantly set out on the 19th for Neapolitan waters. He was still suffering from the effects of
his head wound and from perpetual headaches and
vomitings. The voyage, prolonged by the derelict state
of his flagship, acted as an enforced holiday.

On September 22nd 1798, towed ironically by a
frigate, the *Vanguard* anchored off Naples. 'I hope,'
Nelson wrote to Sir William Hamilton, 'to be no more
than four or five days at Naples, for these are not times

for idleness.' He had reckoned without the ambassador's lady. Accompanied by the King and Queen of Naples, this large, fascinating, vulgar, dynamic woman of thirty-three bore down on the Admiral with the same spirit that he himself had borne down on the French. She had only set eyes on him once before when, five years earlier during the siege of Toulon, he had borne dispatches to Naples. But she was resolved to conquer him as he had conquered Brueys. Acknowledged as a mistress of dramatic effect—her 'attitudes' were the talk of the less exacting *salons* of Europe—she positively boarded the unsophisticated sailor on his own quarterdeck. Still bemused from that astonishing encounter he described it in a letter three days later to his wife. 'Up flew her ladyship and exclaiming, "O God, is it possible?" she fell into my arm more dead than alive.' She was followed by the King who, seizing the admiral by the hand, hailed him as his deliverer and preserver.

It was all too much for Nelson and his poor dazed head. The loveliest city of southern Europe was in summer gala to receive him, the most voluptuous of women at his feet. After the strain and intense excitement of the summer and the dreary reaction of the voyage west, he could not refrain from yielding to all this overflow of tenderness and adulation. It seemed a sailor's due, after the hardships and deprivations of the sea. He had known little of luxury and nothing of Courts. He found himself when he was least able to withstand its fatal charm the adored hero of the most luxurious and enervating society in existence. He struggled for a little while : wrote to St. Vincent a week after his arrival that he was in a country of fiddlers, puppets and scoundrels : that it was a dangerous place for a simple sailor and he must keep clear of it. A fortnight later he sailed for Malta, where the islanders had risen against the French garrison at the first news of the Nile, to organise a blockade of Valetta. But he left his heart behind in Naples, and early in November, at the first stirrings of Continental war, he returned there to be the counsellor of an admiring king and queen and the hero of a lovely and designing woman, and to waste his genius in an element alien to it.

　　　　　　•　　　•　　　•

It was not until Monday, October 1st, exactly two months after the battle that the postscript of *Lloyd's Evening Post* announced that the Hamburg mail had arrived with news of a glorious victory in which Admiral Nelson had destroyed or captured all but two of the French battleships. Next morning Captain Capel of the *Mutine* delivered Nelson's dispatches to the Admiralty. Within a few minutes the Park and Tower guns began to fire and all the church bells to peal. And as the steeples started to rock, the wife of the First Lord sat down to write to the hero of England. 'Joy, joy, joy to you, brave, gallant, immortal Nelson! May the great God whose cause you so valiantly support, protect and bless you to the end of your brilliant career. . . . My heart is absolutely bursting with different sensations of joy, of gratitude, of pride, of every emotion that ever warmed the bosom of a British woman on hearing of her country's glory.'

There was scarcely anybody in England who did not realise the magnitude of the victory. The *Annual Register* described it as 'the most signal that had graced the British Navy since the days of the Spanish Armada.' The old King, when the despatch reached him at Weymouth, read Nelson's opening words, then stopped and, standing silent for a minute, turned his eyes to heaven. It seemed to promise not only a lasting salvation for England, but preservation from anarchy, distress and misery for the still free countries of Europe, liberation for the enslaved, and, in the fullness of time, peace.

CHAPTER THREE

THE BATTLE OF THE BALTIC

'Of Nelson and the North sing the glorious
day's renown.'

Campbell

The two years which followed Nelson's arrival at Naples
after his victory of the Nile were in some ways the sad-
dest in his life and blemished his wonderful reputation
and career. Desperately in love with Lady Hamilton—a
once fabulously lovely woman whose beauty was now
fast fading and who, with her melodramatic nature, was
resolved to keep her last lover and hero constantly at
her side—he appeared everywhere with her and her
ageing husband, the ambassador. At her instigation he
became involved in the treacherous politics of the cor-
rupt Neapolitan court. It was his nature to do everything
with passionate intensity, and for a time his devotion to
her almost took the place of his utter dedication to his
country's service. On one occasion, in his anxiety to
defend Naples and Sicily against attack, he even ignored
a superior's order and incurred the displeasure of the
Admiralty. In the summer of 1800, pleading wounds
and illness, he resigned his command and returned
home. Travelling across Europe with the Hamiltons, he
was everywhere lionised as a hero, with his adored
Emma beside him. But when he reached England,
though his carriage was drawn by a cheering mob from
Ludgate to the Guildhall and the City fathers presented him with a diamond-studded sword, his wife
refused to countenance his new friends and parted from

him for ever, while the King, after the briefest of greetings, turned his back on him at a levée. In political and official circles it was assumed by many that his career was finished.

From this sad state of affairs Nelson was retrieved by the call of duty. The great European coalition against Revolutionary France, which had been brought about by his victory at the Nile, had by now been defeated by the genius of General Bonaparte who, having escaped from Egypt and evaded the British blockade, had made himself First Consul and dictator of France. Even Russia turned against Britain and, joining with the maritime powers of Denmark and Sweden in a Confederacy of the North, closed the Baltic to her trade, cutting off the supplies of naval stores and grain on which her fleets and the factory population of her new industrial towns largely depended.

Faced with the closure of the ports of all Europe against her and by a threat of famine, Britain's rulers did not hesitate. Gathering every available warship in home waters, the Government assembled early in 1801 a fleet at Yarmouth for immediate service in the Baltic. Its command was entrusted to a sixty-two-year-old admiral, Sir Hyde Parker, who possessed more seniority than experience of active service and was known to the Navy as 'old vinegar'. But to spur him to action, the Admiralty appointed as second-in-command the youngest and most daring Vice-Admiral in the Service, the forty-two-year-old Lord Nelson of the Nile.

The effect on Nelson was electric. 'We are now arrived,' he wrote to a friend, 'at that period we have often heard of but must now execute—that of fighting for our dear country.' He reached Yarmouth on March 6th, flying his flag in the *St. George*. He found his elderly admiral 'a little nervous about dark nights and fields of ice'. 'We must brace up,' he reported, 'these are not times for nervous systems. I hope we shall give our northern enemies that hailstorm of bullets which gives our dear country the domination of the seas. All the devils in the north cannot take it from us if our wooden walls have fair play.' For Nelson viewed England's new enemies with the same pugnacity and intensity as the old. 'Down, down with the French!' had been his repeated cry in the Mediterranean, and he now applied it to their allies. 'I am afraid,' he had once truly written of himself, 'I take all my services too much to heart.'

Sir Hyde, worthy man, did not. His chief interest at the moment was a farewell ball which his young wife was preparing to give at Yarmouth on March 13th. Nelson, knowing that every minute was precious if the Baltic Powers were to be disarmed in detail before they had time to prepare and unite their forces, was beside himself with impatience. 'Strike home and quick,' he urged. He dropped a hint of Parker's preoccupation to his old friend, St. Vincent, now called to the Admiralty. Whereupon the fleet received orders to sail at once, the ball was abandoned and the two admirals started on their mission on decidedly strained terms.

But when Nelson made up his mind, there was no resisting him. Between the sailing of the fleet on March 12th and its arrival on the 19th at the Skaw, the northernmost point of Denmark, he had already half won over his superior—tradition has it with a timely turbot. There was something about Nelson's ardour and, when his imagination was aroused, his limitless dedication to his country's service that touched even the dullest heart.

Not that he had yet succeeded in inspiring Parker

with his own spirit. Eighteen miles north of Krönborg
Castle and Helsingor (Elsinore), where the Kattegat
narrows into the Sound between Sweden and the Danish
island of Zealand, the fleet anchored to await the return
of Nicholas Vansittart, the Government envoy, who had
been sent on in a frigate to Copenhagen with a 48-hour
ultimatum. Nelson was for pushing on at once into the
Baltic before the Danes and their Russian and Swedish
allies were ready. But until Vansittart had a chance to
accomplish his mission Parker would not face the double
guns of the Elsinore Straits and the responsibility for
precipitating war with countries still technically neutral.
Nelson's strong, realist mind told him diplomacy was
now useless, that the Danes having gone so far would
not draw back without the compulsion of force and that
they would merely use the delay to make themselves
stronger. Every minute lost meant the certain death of
more brave men and the endangering of England's
purpose.

It was a sombre moment. The weather was bitterly
cold and half the fleet seemed to be coughing. On March
23rd Vansittart returned with the Crown Prince of
Denmark's rejection of the British ultimatum. Nelson
was thereupon summoned to the flagship. 'Now we are
sure of fighting,' he wrote to Lady Hamilton, 'I am sent
for!' He found all in the deepest gloom, Vansittart
expatiating on the strength of the Danish defences, and
Parker, appalled by his account of great batteries erected
by multitudes of defiant Danes, in favour of anchoring
in the Kattegat till the united Baltic navies emerged to
give battle. Nelson thereupon set to work, quietly and
cheerfully, to argue the Council of War round : 'to
bring,' as he put it, 'people to the post.' Pacing up and
down the flagship's stateroom he pressed his reasons for

attacking and, lucidly, persuasively, yet with a flame
which shamed all fears, showed how it might be done.
After learning that the Copenhagen defences were in
the north where the Trekronor Battery barred the
approach from the Sound, he suggested that the fleet
should follow the longer route by the Great Belt round
Zealand and so fall on the enemy where he was least
expecting attack, in the rear. The manoeuvre would
have had the additional advantage of placing the British
between the Danes and their Russian and Swedish allies.
But the great thing, he insisted, was to attack at once.
'Go by the Sound or by the Belt or anyhow,' he said,
'only lose not an hour.'

It was not Nelson's habit to leave anything to chance.
He had talked the Council round, but as soon as he
returned to his ship he sat down to write a long letter to
Parker emphasising the reasons for action. This document, dated March 24th, was the very quintessence of
Nelson : daring, sagacious, winning. 'The more I have
reflected, the more I am confirmed in the opinion that
not a moment should be lost in attacking the enemy.
They will every day and hour be stronger; we shall
never be so good a match for them as at this moment.
. . . By Mr. Vansittart's account their state of preparation exceeds what he conceives our Government thought
possible, and the Danish Government is hostile to us in
the greatest possible degree. Therefore here you are,
with almost the safety, certainly with the honour, of
England more entrusted to you than ever yet fell to the
lot of any British officer. On your decision depends
whether our Country shall be degraded in the eyes of
Europe or whether she shall rear her head higher than
ever . . . I am of the opinion the boldest measures are
the safest.'

Parker's yielding nature could not resist such strength. He would not, as Nelson urged, press boldly on against the Russians—the heart of the Armed League—and smash half their fleet at Reval while it was still separated from the remainder by the ice. The thought of leaving the Danish ships in his rear was too much for his conventional mind. But he agreed to pass through the Belt and attack the Danes : on that point he argued no more. On the 26th, as soon as the wind allowed, the fleet weighed and steered towards the Belt. But on learning from his flag-captain something of the danger of those intricate waters, the admiral changed his mind and decided to brave what he had refused before, the narrow entrance to the Sound between the Danish and Swedish guns. As often happens when men boldly grapple with difficulties, the initial obstacles vanished as soon as tackled. When, after being detained by head winds for three days, the fleet entered the dreaded Straits of Elsinore on the 30th, the passage proved absurdly easy. Finding little opposition from the Swedish shore, where the batteries of Krönborg were not yet ready, the ships inclined to the east of the channel and sailed southward with the Danish shot splashing harmlessly short of it.

That afternoon eighteen British sail of the line and thirty-five smaller vessels anchored five miles south of Copenhagen. The two admirals at once made an inspection of the town's defences in a schooner. They found that they had been still further strengthened during the days of waiting. But Nelson showed no sign of dismay. 'It looks formidable,' he wrote to Emma Hamilton, 'to those who are children at war, but to my judgment with ten sail of the line I think I can annihilate them; at all events I hope I shall be allowed to try.'

Next day at the Council of War he got his way, and, when he asked for ten battleships, Parker gave him twelve. The old gentleman, in spite of his longing for ease and quiet, was almost coming to love Nelson.

How great was the need for speed was shown on the day the British passed the Sound. A hundred miles away Danish troops entered the Free Town of Hamburg, while the Prussians, scenting plunder, cast in their lot with the Baltic Powers and closed the mouths of the Elbe, Ems and Weser to British commerce. A few days later they invaded Hanover, the hereditary domain of King George III. Hesitation at that hour would have been fatal. England could only hold her place now in the world by courage and resolution.

At a second Council of War Nelson's plan was adopted for the destruction of the Danish fleet and floating batteries. About two miles to the east of Copenhagen the water in front of the city was broken by a great shoal known to pilots as the Middle Ground. Between this and the short flats ran a swift current of deep water called the King's Channel. Along its western or inner side were anchored nineteen hulks and floating batteries with a host of smaller vessels in an unbroken line whose head was protected by the famous Trekronor Battery. Instead of attacking it from its strongest end, Nelson proposed to take the twelve lightest battleships and the smaller vessels of the fleet round the Middle Ground and so sweep up the King's Channel from the south with the current. This would enable him, after crippling the enemy, to rejoin the rest of the fleet without turning. It involved, however, an intricate and dangerous piece of navigation, for the shoal waters round the Middle Ground ran like a mill race, and the fleet had no charts. But Nelson spent the icy, foggy nights of March 30th and 31st in an open boat taking soundings, and he felt confident of his ability to take the battle fleet through the shoals. It was by now his only chance of overcoming the defences.

While Parker with the reserve moved up to the north end of the Middle Ground about four miles from the city, Nelson, on the afternoon of April 1st, skirted the west of the shoal and anchored at sundown some two miles to the south of the Danish line. That night he entertained his captains on board his temporary flagship, the *Elephant*—for the *St. George* was too large for his business—and afterwards, exhausted by his efforts of the past two nights, lay in his cot for several hours dictating orders, while his flag-captain, Hardy, took soundings round the head of the Danish line. Nelson's instructions, unlike those issued before the Nile, were of the most detailed kind. There would be no room for manoeuvring on the morrow and little for individual initiative. Every ship was therefore allotted an exact task.

During the night the wind veered to the south as though to reward Nelson for his pains. He was up long before dawn making final preparations. At eight the captains came aboard for their final orders : at nine-thirty the fleet weighed. At the last moment the pilots panicked; masters of small Baltic traders, the thought of taking great battleships through such narrow, shallow waters was too much for them. In the subsequent confusion three of the four leading ships—or a quarter of the main British force—went aground. Disaster was only averted by Nelson's promptitude in putting the *Elephant*'s helm a-starboard and so bringing her past the grounded *Russell* into the main channel which the pilots had lost. The rest of the fleet, following him, steered clear of the shoal.

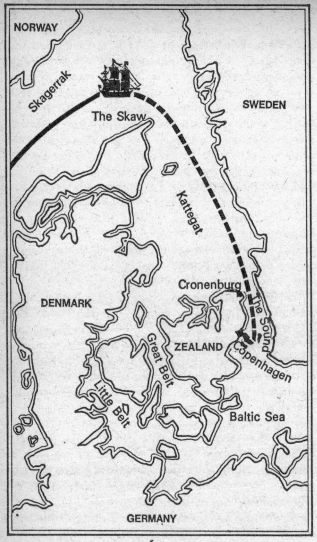

The route of the English fleet to Copenhagen

As usual the British entered action without a sound. Both sides seemed to be awed by the solemnity of the scene : the great ships like enormous white birds, with rows of cannon bristling beneath their canvas, bearing down on the Danish line, and the waiting city tense with expectation. In that brooding silence the chant of the pilot and helmsman sounded to one listening midshipman like the responses in a cathedral service. Then, as the leading ship came into range of the enemy batteries, the thunder began. For nearly four hours the Danes, with successive relays of volunteers from the shore taking the place of the fallen, kept up the cannonade. Along a mile and a half of water, with only a cable's length between them, fifteen hundred guns pounded away at one another : 'I have been in a hundred and five engagements,' wrote Nelson, 'but that of today is the most terrible of them all.'

Twice the Danish Commodore was forced to shift his flag; in the *Dannebrog*, 270 of the crew of 336 were struck down. One or two of the British ships endured casualties almost as heavy : the *Monarch* lost over two hundred men. 'Hard pounding,' remarked Nelson to Colonel Stewart of the Rifle Corps, 'but mark you, I would not be anywhere else for a thousand pounds.' At one moment Parker, seeing from his distant anchorage that three of the British ships were aground, flew the signal 'Cease Action'.

But Nelson, knowing that to break off at such a moment would be disastrous, disregarded it, symbolically putting his telescope to his blind eye. 'Keep mine for closer battle still flying,' he said, 'Nail it to the mast.' Only the frigates, which under Captain Riou had taken the place of the grounded battleships in front of the Trekronor Battery, noticed Parker's signal. Unable to see

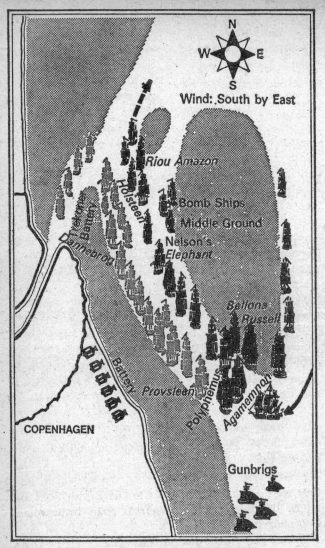

Plan of the Battle of Copenhagen

Nelson's and all but blown out of the water, they sadly broke off the engagement. 'What,' cried Riou, 'will Nelson think of us?' Almost as he spoke a raking shot cut him in half.

About two o'clock in the afternoon, the Danes' fire slackened. Taken at a disadvantage by the unexpected direction of the attack, and, for all their courage, over-borne by the deadly accuracy of the British fire, they could do no more. Nelson's own position was almost as precarious, with the undefeated Trekronor batteries dominating the treacherous channel between his battered ships and the main fleet to northward. With the sure psychological insight which was part of his greatness, he at once penned a letter addressed : 'To the brothers of Englishmen, the Danes,' and sent it under a flag of truce to the Crown Prince. For his instinct told him that he could now obtain what he came for without further bloodshed.

The weariness of his foes and his glorious bluff did the rest. While he referred the terms of the proposed armistice back to the *London,* he cleared his ships from the shoals under the silent guns of the Trekronor batteries and drew off his prizes. His reputation as much as his crew's gunnery had broken the enemy's will to resist. And, thanks to his exquisite skill as a negotiator, the truce, prolonged from day to day, ended in a permanent armistice. The Danes were to suspend their alliance with the Russians and leave their warships in their existing unmasted state for fourteen weeks, during which time they were to supply provisions to the British fleet. In return the British were to refrain from bombarding Copenhagen.

Nelson had gained his purpose. The hands of Denmark were tied, and his admiral was free to proceed

against the Russians without fear for his rear. On April
12th the fleet entered the Baltic. But to Nelson's disgust,
instead of proceeding to Reval with a fair wind Parker
waited off the Swedish coast for new instructions from
England. A blow at Russia, Nelson saw, would destroy
the whole northern Coalition, for Denmark and Sweden
were merely intimidated by their mighty neighbour.
And so long as the ice in the Gulf of Finland prevented
the Russian squadron at Reval from retiring on its inner
base at Kronstadt, Britain by striking could either destroy
it or exact terms from the Tsar. When Parker objected
that too rapid an advance up the Baltic might expose
the whole fleet to a superior Russian and Swedish combination, Nelson replied: 'I wish they were twice as
many: the more numerous, the easier the victory!' For
he knew that their inability to manoeuvre in large
bodies would place them at his mercy.

Not till May 5th did fresh instructions arrive from
England. They recalled Parker and left Nelson in command. Immediately the latter left for Reval, but too late.
Three days before, the ice had melted sufficiently to
enable the threatened Russian squadron to retreat to
Kronstadt. There was nothing for Nelson to do but to
make as firm and dignified an exchange of letters with
the Tsar's Minister, Count Pahlen, as circumstances
admitted, and then retire.

But his work, if incomplete, was done. The shattering
effect of the Battle of Copenhagen, coupled with the
Tsar Paul's death, had destroyed Bonaparte's prestige
throughout the North. On hearing the news he expressed
his feelings by stamping and shouting with rage. The
new Tsar, Alexander, like his subjects, had no wish to
preserve a quarrel with a former ally of such strength
and courage as Britain. When Nelson went ashore at

Reval, the populace hailed him with cries of 'That is him! that is him!—the young Suvorof!' 'The Baltic people will never fight me if it is to be avoided,' he commented. On May 16th 1801, Russia raised her embargo on British ships, and a month later a Convention between the two countries affirmed the full legality both of the right of search and the seizure of hostile goods in neutral bottoms. Already Prussia and Denmark had withdrawn their troops from Hanover and Hamburg. The northern threat to Britain's security was at an end.

The tidings of Nelson's victory filled the country with relief. For the second time he became the hero of England: 'Your Lordship's whole conduct,' wrote St. Vincent, 'is the subject of our constant admiration. It does not become me to make comparisons: all agree there is but one Nelson.'

CHAPTER FOUR

THE PURSUIT OF VILLENEUVE

'The wind was rising easterly, the morning sky
was blue,
The Straits before us opened wide and free;
We looked towards the Admiral where high the
Peter flew,
And all our hearts were dancing like the sea.
"The French are gone to Martinique with four-
and-twenty sail."
The old *Superb* is old and frail and slow,
But the French are gone to Martinique and
Nelson's on the trail,
And where he goes the old *Superb* must go!'

Newbolt

In the winter after Nelson's victorious return from the
Baltic, Great Britain and France—the one supreme on
land, the other at sea—made a truce. The makeshift
Peace of Amiens meant for Nelson release from a pur-
poseless task, for, though in the face of an invasion scare
he had been appointed to command a defence flotilla in
the English Channel he knew that invasion-barges
would never be able to cross the Straits of Dover un-
escorted. For the next year he lived with the Hamiltons
at Merton in Surrey where he had bought a home to
share with them. In April 1803, Sir William died, leaving him in sole possession of Emma and of the child,
Horatia, which she had secretly borne him. His happiness was shortlived, for a month later war broke out
again and he was immediately recalled to service. On
May 18th he hoisted his flag in the *Victory* and two
days later sailed for the Mediterranean to take supreme
command there.

His instructions were couched in the broadest terms, for, once on his station, no orders from England could reach him under many weeks. He was to maintain watch over the French fleet at Toulon, prevent its union with the Spaniards should the latter show signs of activity, and protect Malta, Naples, Sicily, the Ionian Islands and the Turkish dominions in Europe, Asia and Africa. He was also to keep the Mediterranean and Aegean clear of French privateers and Algerian pirates. He had no ally—for the Two Sicilies and Sardinia, though secretly friendly, were far too terrified of France to offer him active help—and no base nearer than Malta and Gibraltar, respectively seven hundred and nine hundred miles from his station off Toulon. His task was complicated by the fact that his ships could not, like those of the Channel Fleet, put into Plymouth or Portsmouth to refit, but, however rotten, had to remain on the station till they could be replaced from England. 'If I am to watch the French,' he wrote in a Gulf of Lyons gale, 'I must be at sea; and if at sea must have bad weather; and if the ships are not fit to stand bad weather, they are useless.' For by discharging highly-skilled if over-leisurely workmen from the yards during the Peace, selling off surplus stores and discouraging the allocation of contracts to private shipbuilders, the Admiralty had seriously handicapped the Navy. Collingwood reported at Christmas 1803 that his ship's company was worked to death to right defects in a vessel which proved unfit for sea. 'We have been sailing,' he wrote, 'for the last six months with only a sheet of copper between us and eternity.'

Only Nelson's inexhaustible resource enabled Britain to maintain her Mediterranean blockade at all. Dependent for supplies on the neutral islands of Sardinia and

Sicily—neither of which was safe from French attack—
and on a Spain which, lying athwart his communications, might at any moment enter the war against him,
the British Admiral's position was one of growing
jeopardy. The whole Italian mainland was under
French control, with St. Cyr's army waiting in Calabria
to pounce on Sicily, Greece or Egypt.

From his first arrival, therefore, Nelson repeatedly
appealed to London for troops to protect Sicily and
Sardinia. 'I have made up my mind.' he told Lady
Hamilton, 'that it is part of the plan of that Corsican
scoundrel to conquer the Kingdom of Naples. . . . If the
poor king remonstrates, he will call it a war and declare
a conquest.' The only certain remedy was to forestall
him by occupying Messina. But the Government at
home was too concerned with securing England against
invasion to spare the troops. It even recalled from Malta
the last remnants of the small but well-trained army
with which Abercromby had conquered Egypt two years
before.

Beyond Sicily was the Levant and the misgoverned
provinces of the Ottoman Empire. Here was a vacuum
at the point where Europe opened on to Asia. And
though Napoleon's sea passage to the Levant was barred
by Nelson's fleet, there was an alternative route along
the shores of the Adriatic and Aegean. With Austria's
neutrality secured, a Franco-Russian partition of the
Balkans might turn the whole British position in the
Orient. 'I cannot help thinking,' wrote Nelson, 'that
Russia and France understand each other about the
Turkish dominions. If so, Egypt will be the price.' And
Egypt, guarding the door to Africa and the overland
route to India, Napoleon had once described as the most
important country in the world.

The British had needed the Peace of Amiens for trade; Napoleon in order to prepare to conquer the world. Emperor now of the French and absolute ruler of western Europe, he assembled a vast army on the Channel shore and started to mobilise the fleets of the Continent to break the British blockade. On July 2nd 1804, he ordered his finest Admiral, Latouche-Tréville, to give Nelson the slip, and, escaping from Toulon into the Atlantic, release the French ships from Cadiz and Rochefort, make a wide sweep round Cornwallis's blockading force off Brest and, either rounding the British Isles or running straight up Channel, appear off Boulogne in September with sixteen sail of the line and eleven frigates. 'Let us,' he wrote, 'be masters of the Straits for six hours and we shall be masters of the world.'

But Latouche-Tréville never got out into the Atlantic because Nelson made it impossible for him to do so without fighting. Unable to remain close to the port in the Gulf of Lyons gales, the fiery little admiral tried not so much to hold him in Toulon as to lure him out. He offered him every opportunity to put to sea, believing that once he had got him there he would make it impossible for him to do further harm. 'If we could get fairly alongside,' he wrote, 'I daresay there would be some spare hats by the time we had done.' This, however, was not at all what the French wanted : their object was to reach the Atlantic and Channel uncrippled and without an action. Once that summer, encouraged by Nelson's trick of keeping his main fleet over the horizon, Latouche-Tréville edged out of port with eight sails of the line and gave chase to the British frigates. After pursuing for a few miles he realised that he was running into a trap and returned to harbour. A report of the episode in the Paris Press—the only fruit of Napoleon's first naval design—almost reduced Nelson to an apoplexy. 'You will have seen Monsier Latouche's letter,' he wrote, 'of how he chased me and how I ran. I keep it, and, by God, if I take him, he shall eat it!' A few weeks later he had his revenge when, worn out by over-much climbing to the Sepet signal-post to watch the British fleet, Latouche-Tréville died of heart-failure. 'I always said that would be his death,' observed Nelson.

Even had Latouche-Tréville lived and contrived to escape Nelson, he could not have evaded Cornwallis's Western Squadron. The ultimate function of the great British fighting force off Ushant was not, as Napoleon, like other landsmen supposed, merely to blockade Brest but to secure the approaches to the English and Irish Channels. Absolute blockade of a port, especially in winter, was impossible : sooner or later fog or gale was sure to offer a chance of escape. British naval strategy aimed rather at making it impossible for any French fleet or combination of fleets to enter the Channel without having to fight a superior or equal force. For the Western Approaches were the key to England's existence. Through these waters passed and repassed the merchant shipping on which depended her wealth, drawn from every corner of the earth : the great convoys or 'trades' which it was the unsleeping task of the Navy to secure. As they neared the danger zone close to the French ports the arms of the Western Squadron reached out to protect them. Its frigate tentacles, stretching far out into the outer ocean and southward beyond the Bay, could feel every movement of a converging foe long before he reached the Soundings.

In a series of world wars extending over more than sixty years British seamen had been engaged in thwarting every conceivable combination of hostile navies. The task had become second nature to them, and there was scarcely a senior officer who had not mastered every move of the game. Such men were not likely to forget their business merely because an amateur of genius took to mapping out the sea in his cabinet at St. Cloud as though it were the Lombardy Plain. On August 24th 1804 the Admiralty issued instructions adapting the classic strategy of Britain—the 'matured tradition' of more than two centuries—to the needs of the hour. The French Brest fleet, Cornwallis was warned, sailing without troops, might try to enter the Channel and cover the passage of the Grand Army to Kent. If it evaded him, he was to fall back on the Lizard ready to follow it in any direction. Since it would be suicide for its commander, Ganteaume, to enter the Channel with an undefeated fleet in his rear, it seemed more likely that his destination would be Ireland or Sicily. Any large embarkation of troops would suggest one or other of these, and a smaller the West Indies. Cornwallis was therefore to be ready to detach a division in pursuit, while keeping sufficient force in the Bay to meet any attempt of the enemy to double back on the Channel.

Possibly Napoleon had already divined this, though he refused to admit it to his admirals and the world. Having reaffirmed his faith in his destiny before Charlemagne's tomb at Aix, he drew up a new plan against the English. Realising that they might make the task of his scattered squadrons progressively harder as they neared their destination, he sought instead to lure them away from the entrance to the Channel. Sailing at the end of October for diversionary raids on the West Indies and South Atlantic trade routes, the Toulon and Rochefort squadrons were to present the greedy islanders with the alternative of losing the wealth of their colonies and trade or of uncovering their heart. Having drawn half their fleet away on wild-goose chases, the two French admirals were to double back to support Ganteaume, who was to escape from Brest in November, land 18,000 shock troops in Ireland and, running up Channel or rounding Cape Wrath according to the wind, convoy either Marmont's 25,000 from the Texel to Ireland or the Grand Army from Boulogne to Kent. In either case the war would then be won.

For the moment the logic of sea power was forcing Napoleon back on a policy of action not against England's heart but against the circumference from which he imagined she drew her strength. All over the world were British trading stations and richly laden merchantmen whose only protection was the thin wooden crust of the blockade along the western and southern seaboard of Europe. There was so much to defend that Britain's naval resources appeared insufficient for the task. Spain's entry into the war now further narrowed her dwindling margin of safety. By a treaty signed in Madrid on January 4th 1805, Napoleon secured the promise of thirty-two Spanish ships of the line by the spring. Till they were ready Spain, with her position athwart England's trade routes, afforded a splendid springboard for diversionary raids into the western and southern Atlantic.

Spurred on by their master's orders and aided by winter gales, the commanders of the Rochefort and Toulon squadrons sailed on their West Indian mission. Missiessy, with 3,500 troops packed in his five battle-ships and attendant cruisers, escaped from Rochefort in a snowstorm on January 11th 1805. A week later Latouche-Tréville's successor, Villeneuve, put out from

Lady Hamilton: this portrait by Schmidt was Nelson's
favourite and hung in his cabin

Action at the height of the battle of Trafalgar

Nelson's sleeping cot on board the *Victory*

A romantic painting of Nelson leaving Portsmouth
for the last time, bound for Trafalgar

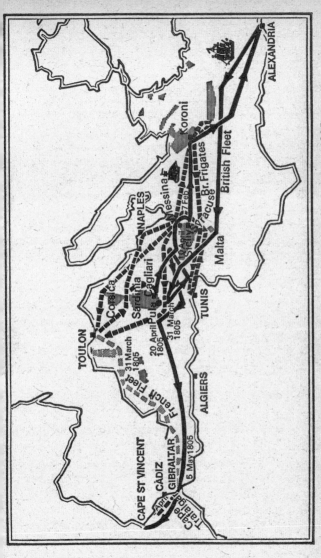

The hunt for Villeneuve round the Mediterranean, 1805

D

Toulon with eleven of the line and nine cruisers. Nelson,
who had been praying for him to come out, was victualling in Maddalena Bay when his frigates brought the
news. In three hours he was under way, leading his ships
in a north-westerly gale through the dangerous Biche
passage and standing along the eastern coast of Sardinia for Cagliari. With the wind hauling every minute
more into the west, he had three main anxieties—
Sardinia, the Two Sicilies, and Egypt, for he knew that
the French had embarked troops. On the 26th, battered
by the gale, he reached Cagliari to learn that no landing
had been made. He at once sailed with the wind for
Palermo to save Naples and Sicily.

For Nelson's duty was clear. Only by preventing the
enemy from invading the neutral countries of the central
and eastern Mediterranean could he maintain the command of that sea on which Pitt's plans for the offensive
depended. From this strategic principle nothing could
deflect him, not even his longing for glory and an early
return to his mistress and daughter. Aching to meet the
enemy, he continued to put first things first. 'I would
willingly have half of mine burnt to effect their destruction,' he wrote on January 25th 1805, 'I am in a fever;
God send I may find them!' But he refused to uncover
the vital point that he had been sent to defend, and kept
his eastward course for Sicily.

By the 20th Nelson knew that the island key to the
central Mediterranean was safe. The French had made
no attempt to attack Neapolitan territory. With the prevailing westerly gales they must either have put back
into Toulon or sailed ahead of him, as in '98, to Egypt
or Greece. To secure the Turkish provinces and the
overland route to Egypt, he therefore pressed on
through the Straits of Messina towards the Morea and

Alexandria. Here on February 7th, as he had predicted, he found the Turks unprepared, the fortifications unmanned and the garrison asleep. With a week's start, he told the Governor of Malta, the French would have made the place impregnable.

But the latter, as he had guessed, were back in Toulon. Three days of storm and the fear of the victor of the Nile had been too much for Villeneuve and his untrained crews. 'These gentlemen,' wrote Nelson, who in twenty-one months had never set foot on shore or lost a spar, 'are not accustomed to a Gulf of Lyons gale. . . . Bonaparte has often made his boast that our fleet would be worn out by keeping at sea and that his was kept in order and increasing by staying in port. But I fancy, that his fleet suffers more in a night than ours in a year.' On March 22nd Napoleon again sent urgent orders to Villeneuve to sail by the 26th. His instructions reached the latter on that day. Four days later the unhappy officer stole out of Toulon at dead of night with eleven battleships and eight cruisers. He was speeded by two fears—of his master behind and of Nelson lurking beyond him watching frigates on the horizon. The 'fiery admiral', as the French called him, had been reported off Barcelona on March 17th, and, instead of hugging the Catalan coast, Villeneuve steered south to avoid him, intending to pass to the east of the Balearics before shaping course for Cartagena and Cadiz. Without knowing it, he was running straight into Nelson's arms.

For that long-thwarted seaman after his weary return from Egypt had baited a trap. Unable to cover both the Straits and Sicily save by lying close off Toulon—an untenable position in the March gales—he adopted an ingenious expedient. He chose his usual rendezvous in the Gulf of Palmas on the south-west coast of Sardinia to forestall any move towards Sicily and the Levant. But in order to deter Villeneuve from using the one exit he could not block, and tempt him—were his destination the Atlantic—to follow an easterly course, he made a demonstration off the Spanish coast. Then, aware that his quarry was embarking troops, he hurried back to Palmas to await him.

Here the French admiral would have met his fate had not a chance encounter with a Ragusan merchantman on the morning of April 1st put him wise. Learning that Nelson was no longer off Catalonia but almost straight in his course, he turned west and ran for Spain along the north side of the Balearics. He had managed to shake off the shadowing British frigates during the night, and the sudden change of direction prevented them from rediscovering him. He was by now too far to the south to meet the cruiser which his adversary had left off Cape St. Sebastian in case his ruse should fail. Thus, at the very moment for which Nelson had so long waited, the French fleet vanished.

On April 7th Villeneuve anchored off Cartagena and signalled to the warships in the harbour to join him. But the Spaniards, with the gracious dilatoriness of their race, had omitted to load their ammunition and asked for time. Still haunted by the thought of Nelson, Villeneuve refused to wait and sailed with the wind that night. Next morning Lord Mark Kerr, refitting the *Fishgard* frigate in Gibraltar, was startled to see a line of ghostly warships scudding through the Straits before an easterly gale. Vice-Admiral Orde and his five blockading battleships off Cadiz had just time to withdraw as Villeneuve's nineteen ships rose over the eastern horizon. Anchoring outside Cadiz Bay at eight o'clock on the morning of April 9th, Villeneuve signalled to the single French warship and as many of the fifteen Spanish battleships as were ready for sea to join him at once. Soon after noon he gave the order to weigh and by nightfall was receding into the west with six belated Spaniards straggling after him. When Orde's cruisers reappeared off Cadiz next day the Combined Fleet had disappeared, no one knew where.

Meanwhile Nelson had been passing through a period of strain and frustration worse than any since his chase of Napoleon in 1798. On the night of March 31st when his frigates lost sight of Villeneuve, he was waiting off the Sardinian coast for the reward of his labours. 'We have had a very dull war,' he told a friend, 'it must now be changed for a more active one.' But on the morning of April 4th he learnt that the French had again escaped him. He had no idea where they had gone and, true to his unfailing principle, refused to act till he could base action on judgment. Instead he took his station midway between Sardinia and the African coast in order to cover that island and the vital objectives to the east. 'I shall neither go to the eastward of Sicily nor to the westward of Sardinia,' he wrote, 'until I know something positive.'

For twelve days he remained cruising between the two islands without the slightest news. Owing to a series of mischances no instructions had reached him from England of later date than November. At that time the position in India had seemed very grave, and he was therefore acutely conscious of the possibility of a new attempt on Egypt—a consciousness which Napoleon had done all in his power to foster by troop movements and false Press reports.

But, as day after day passed and the silence continued, Nelson's mind began to misgive him. On the morning of April 10th while cruising near Palermo he learnt by chance that a military expedition had left or was about to leave England for Malta to co-operate with a Russian force in Italy. At once his quick perception warned him of the worst. Villeneuve, evading his outlook off Cape St. Sebastian, had sailed to the west, not the east, with the express object of intercepting the convoy. It seemed inconceivable to Nelson that as Commander-in-Chief in the Mediterranean he had not been warned to protect it. Yet it was just the kind of muddle that British Governments made.

He at once began to beat back to the west. But the wind was now dead in his teeth. In nine days he only covered two hundred miles. 'My fortune seems flown away,' he bemoaned. 'I cannot get a fair wind or even a side wind. Dead foul!' On the 18th he learnt from a passing merchantman that the French had been seen off the Spanish coast eleven days before, sailing west. Next day confirmation arrived that they had passed the Straits, been joined by the Spaniards in Cadiz and had sailed again without entering the harbour.

Agonised though he was, Nelson at once made up his mind. As the Spanish Admiral Gravina had joined Villeneuve, he guessed that the object must be something more than a buccaneering raid against the sugar islands. It must be either Ireland or the Channel. He therefore informed the Admiralty that he was sailing at once for the Atlantic, proposing a rendezvous west of the Scillies where his fleet could join in the defence of the British Isles. 'I shall bring with me,' he added, 'eleven as fine ships of war, as ably commanded and in as perfect order and health, as ever went to sea.' It was his one consolation.

With his almost fretful care for all contingencies he

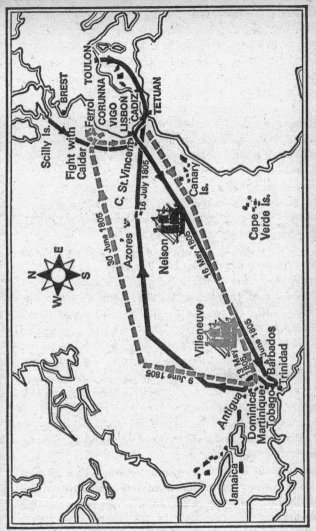

The chase to the West Indies

left five of his much needed frigates to guard the Two Sicilies. Then he bent once more to the task of getting up the Mediterranean. Battling against head-winds and squally weather, in two successive days he made only fifteen miles. For nearly a month the monotonous struggle continued, while his heart all but broke. 'O French fleet, French fleet,' he wrote, 'if I can but once get up with you, I'll make you pay dearly for all you made me suffer!' Yet, though he poured out his heart in his letters to Emma, he relaxed no effort. 'I am not made to despair,' he told Lord Melville; 'what man can do shall be done.'

Not till May 4th did he reach Tetuan Bay. Here all hands were set to work getting in provisions and water. On the 5th the wind came fair and the fleet stood over to Gibraltar where it stayed only four hours. While he was waiting for the wind, Nelson weighed every item of intelligence that could indicate the whereabouts and destination of Villeneuve. He still intended to close on the Channel, yet his information was beginning to point to the French having gone to the West Indies. The most significant item was that given by Rear-Admiral Campbell who, while serving with a Portuguese squadron off the Moroccan coast, had seen the Combined Fleet sailing west on April 11th. The evidence was not conclusive, and Nelson could not run to the West Indies on mere surmise. Yet if he did not and the enemy had gone there, the great sugar island of Jamaica might be lost.

In the next twenty-four hours, victualling in Lagos Bay against a long voyage, Nelson reached a momentous decision. On the evening of May 9th one of Orde's frigates reported having spoken two days before with a vessel which had left Spithead on April 27th. At that date nothing had been heard in England of Villeneuve: a homecoming convoy had also been encountered sailing across the Bay serene and unmolested. It seemed, therefore, certain that the immediate destination of the fleet which had left Cadiz on April 9th could not have been the Channel. Nelson now felt sure it was Martinique. Next morning he wrote that his lot was cast and that he was going to the West Indies. 'Although I am late, yet chance may have given them a bad passage and me a good one. I must hope for the best.'

By May 14th Nelson was at Madeira, dipping south to pick up the long, steady trade winds to waft him to his goal. He had left one of his two three-deckers to accompany the convoy past Cartagena and twenty of his twenty-three cruisers with Rear-Admiral Bickerton to patrol the Mediterranean. Now with ten of the line and three frigates he was in pursuit of a fleet three thousand miles away and nearly twice as big as his own. He knew he was taking his professional life in his hands and that gentlemen abed in England were probably already blackguarding him for his prolonged disappearance. But he had weighed the chances carefully in the light of his professional knowledge. If he was wrong and the French had gone elsewhere, he promised the Admiralty he would be back by the end of June—before the enemy even knew he had crossed the Atlantic. In the meantime salt beef with the French fleet, he told his friend Davison, was preferable to roast beef and champagne without.

        c

On the last day of June an unconvoyed merchantman from Dominica brought tidings to England that Villeneuve had reached Martinique on May 16th. It

seemed that no harm had been done beyond an attack
on the Diamond Rock, and Nelson was known to be in
pursuit. But unlike the public, Lord Barham, the new
First Lord of the Admiralty, a lifelong naval adminis-
trator, realised the significance of the news. For as soon
as the fearful Villeneuve heard of Nelson's arrival in
the West Indies he would be sure to sail with all speed
for Europe. He would make either for the Channel or
Cadiz. By the one he would threaten the British Isles,
by the other the military expedition to Malta and the
Mediterranean.

At that moment Cornwallis was holding Ganteaume's
twenty-one battleships in Brest with twenty-two, Admiral
Stirling Missiessy's returned five in Rochefort with an
equal force, and Calder fourteen French and Spanish
ships in Ferrol with twelve. Seven more British capital
ships were in reserve in the Channel ports. Somewhere
in the Atlantic Nelson's ten were in pursuit of
Villeneuve's eighteen. A further eleven were on the West
Indian stations, two were on their way there from
Collingwood's squadron off Cadiz, and one lay on guard
off Naples.

On July 7th Barham drew up a plan by which Cornwallis was to send ten battleships, or nearly half his
force, to Collingwood. To guard against the risk of
Villeneuve making for the Channel instead of Cadiz,
Calder, having shown himself off Ferrol, was to stretch
north-north-west across the Bay with a cloud of outlying
frigates, while Cornwallis, his depleted battle strength
brought up to fifteen by three fresh vessels from
England, was to cruise south-south-west from Ushant
to meet him. If Villeneuve attempted to raise the blockade of either Ferrol or Brest, he would thus risk an
encounter with twenty-seven capital ships—a force

greatly superior to his own. Napoleon's idea that his Brest or Ferrol squadron would be able to join forces with Villeneuve at the crucial point and moment was based on a misunderstanding of naval warfare. For not only would it take time for the blockaded to discover that the blockaders had gone, but any wind favourable for the former would almost certainly be foul for the homecoming fleet.

But Barham's ingenious expedient was unnecessary. On the night of the 7th a sloop from the West Indies anchored at Plymouth with despatches from Nelson. All next day, while the Admiralty clerks were drafting the requisite orders, her commander, Captain Bettesworth, was posting up the Exeter road. Towards midnight his post-chaise rattled over the Charing Cross cobblestones and drew up at the Admiralty door. He brought urgent despatches from Nelson.

The story contained in Bettesworth's wallet was one of unrelenting pursuit, expectation, frustration and renewed pursuit. Nelson had covered the 3,200 miles from the Straits to Barbados in little more than three weeks— an almost record average of 135 miles a day. Officers and men were on short allowance, but no one minded, for after two years of endurance and waiting they believed they were about to meet the enemy. 'We are all half starved,' wrote one of them, 'and otherwise much inconvenienced by being so long away from port, but our recompense is that we are with Nelson.'

At five o'clock on the afternoon of June 4th his fleet had reached Barbados. A fast sloop, sent ahead, had already brought news of its coming. Since Villeneuve's arrival three weeks before, the islands had been in a state of intense excitement : 'a horseman does not come up quick to the door day or night,' wrote Lady Nugent, from Jamaica, 'but I tremble all over.' At the moment Bridgetown was agog with a message from Brigadier-General Brereton at St. Lucia that the Combined Fleet had been seen on May 29th steering south towards Trinidad.

All through the night after his arrival, at the urgent entreaty of the local Commander-in-Chief, Nelson had embarked troops. By ten next morning he was on his way to Trinidad, taking with him two battleships of Cochrane's which he had found in the port. Five hours later he made the signal, 'Prepare for Battle'. As before the Nile every captain knew what was expected of him, for during the Atlantic crossing the tactics to be employed had been repeatedly discussed. No man could do wrong, the Admiral had told them, who laid his ship close on board the enemy and kept it there till the business was over. For though the Combined Fleet was nearly twice as large as his own, Nelson was confident he could annihilate it. 'Mine is compact, theirs unwieldy,' he wrote, 'and, though a very pretty fiddle, I don't believe that either Gravina or Villeneuve know how to play upon it.'

At Tobago, sighted on June 6th, there had been no word of the enemy. Next day, as the fleet approached the Dragon's Mouth, the British outposts on Trinidad, mistaking its sails for Villeneuve's, fired the blockhouse and withdrew into the woods. At the sight, expectation in the oncoming ships hardened into certainty, only to be dashed by an empty roadstead. Brereton's intelligence had proved false. Without wasting an hour Nelson had put about for Grenada and the north. Next day he learnt that his unsuspecting quarry, having captured the Diamond Rock on June 3rd, had still been at Martinique on the 5th. Had he kept his course for that island—less than a hundred miles from Barbados—he would have encountered the man he had sailed so many miles to find. 'But for General Brereton's damned information,' he wrote to his friend, Davison, 'Nelson would have been, living or dead, the greatest man that England ever saw.'

Meanwhile Villeneuve had been in as great a state of apprehension as the planters he had come to ruin. On his arrival at Martinique on May 13th he had found that Missiessy had returned to France. Hoping daily for Ganteaume's appearance and the signal for his own return, he dared not commit himself to any major operation. On June 4th, after three thousand of his men had gone down with sickness, there arrived from France, not Ganteaume, but Magon with two battleships and orders to await the Brest Fleet for five more weeks and then, if there was still no sign of it, to sail for Ferrol, release the French and Spanish force held there by Calder, and with thirty-three sail of the line make for the Straits of Dover. There, he was assured, the Emperor would be waiting with the Grand Army.

As part of this terrifying programme Villeneuve was instructed to fill in his remaining time in the West Indies by capturing as many British islands as possible. With this intention he had sailed next day for Guadeloupe to embark troops for Barbuda, a small and, as he hoped easy, objective in the extreme north of the Leeward Islands. On his way there on June 8th, while Nelson was still three hundred miles to the south, he had had the fortune to encounter a small convoy of sugar ships off the west coast of Antigua. Capturing fourteen of them, he learnt to his consternation that his terrible pursuer had anchored off Barbados four days before. From that moment the risk of missing Ganteaume in

mid-Atlantic became negligible to the French admiral
compared with the infinitely more alarming risk of meeting Nelson. Ordering his frigates to take back the troops
to Guadeloupe and rejoin him in the Azores, he sailed
next morning for Spain and Ferrol.

When Nelson reached Antigua on the 12th he found
that he was four days too late. Once more he was faced
with the task of basing on a few fragmentary wisps of
evidence a decision involving not only his career but
the very existence of his country. If the French had gone
to Jamaica and he did not follow them, Britain's richest
colony would be lost; if they had gone to Europe, every
ship would be needed in the Western Approaches or off
Cadiz. Precipitate action would endanger the islands
and the two hundred sugar ships he had saved by his
timely arrival; yet delay might jeopardise England herself. He was put out of his agony, just as he was about
to return to Dominica, by news that the French troops,
taken a week before from Guadeloupe, were disembarking. This satisfied him that Villeneuve did not intend to
attack Jamaica. His last doubts were removed a few
hours later by the arrival of the *Netley* schooner which
had been escorting the captured convoy. Powerless to
defend his charges against eighteen sail of the line, her
young captain had kept the enemy under observation
as long as he could and then returned to Antigua to
report. When last seen the Combined Fleet, thirty-two
strong, had been crowding away into the north-east.

Once Nelson was sure that his enemy had sailed for
Europe, his course was clear. Whether they were bound
for the Bay or for Cadiz and the Straits, the protection of
his station was his prior duty. 'I am going towards the
Mediterranean after Gravina and Villeneuve,' he wrote
that night, 'and hope to catch them.' Believing that

command of that sea was essential to Napoleon's scheme of world conquest, he had every hope of an action on the southern crossing, preferably close to the Straits where he could look for reinforcements. Yet even before the *Netley* had anchored in St. John's Road, he had despatched the *Curieux* sloop under Captain Bettesworth for England. With her superior speed she would be able to raise the alarm at least a week before Villeneuve could molest the British squadrons in the Bay. Another cruiser Nelson sent direct to Calder off Ferrol. At noon next day, June 13th, after little more than a week in the West Indies, he had sailed himself for Gibraltar.

．　　　．　　　．

The news Bettesworth brought to the Admiralty on the night of July 8th contained more than Nelson's despatches. On June 19th, 900 miles north-north-east of Antigua, he had sighted the Combined Fleet standing to the northward. Its course made it almost certain that its destination was the Bay. Roused from sleep early on the 9th, the First Lord, upbraiding his servants for not waking him sooner, dictated—Admiralty tradition has it while shaving—an order for strengthening the forces between Villeneuve and his goal. Like Nelson's, his intention was purely offensive. The enemy was at sea and must be crippled before he could reach port. It was the only way to safeguard both Britain and the Mediterranean offensive.

On July 17th Nelson made his landfall at Cape St. Vincent, having crossed the Atlantic in thirty-four days or a fortnight quicker than the less experienced Villeneuve. Next day he passed his old friend Collingwood blockading Cadiz and on the 19th anchored in Gibraltar Bay. 'No French fleet,' he wrote in his diary, 'nor any information about them; how sorrowful this makes me!' Still cursing General Brereton, he went ashore for the first time in two years. He still had hopes that Villeneuve, labouring in the Atlantic behind him, might attempt to re-enter the Mediterranean. But he was coming to share Collingwood's belief that his enemy had gone to the northward.

On July 23rd, having revictualled his fleet at Tetuan, Nelson weighed again for the Atlantic. Two days later, while waiting for an easterly breeze off Tarifa, he received a copy of a Lisbon paper with an account of Captain Bettesworth's arrival in England. The wind at that moment freshening, he sailed in such haste that he left his washing behind. He did not even pause to exchange a word with Collingwood as he passed Cadiz. All the way north, delayed by headwinds on the Portuguese coast, he fretted lest the enemy should do his country some injury before he could arrive. 'I feel every moment of this foul wind,' he wrote in his diary on August 3rd, while Barham at the Admiralty was directing orders to him at Gibraltar to return to England, 'I am dreadfully uneasy.'

On the same day Napoleon reached Boulogne to take command of his invasion army. 'They little guess what is in store for them,' he wrote to his Minister of Marine, Decrès. 'If we are masters of the Straits for twelve hours England is no more.' Only one thing was missing—Villeneuve's fleet. 'I can't make out why we have no news from Ferrol,' he added. 'I can't believe Magon never reached him. I am telling Ganteaume by telegraph to keep out in the Bertheaume Road.'

There was not a moment to lose. The intelligence from Germany and Italy was too grave to be disregarded. Pitt's long-maturing plans for a new Coalition against France were coming to fruition; Austria plainly meant business; the Russian armies were marching south to her aid. Before leaving Paris Napoleon had dictated ultimatums to the Courts of Vienna and Naples threatening them with invasion unless all troop movement ceased immediately. They had still to be sent off, and on August 7th, still hoping that his fleets would arrive in time for him to cross the Channel, he ordered them to be held up a few days longer. At the same time he summoned the Imperial Guard to Boulogne.

Next day he countermanded the order. Nelson was reported from Cadiz to be back in Europe and to have been sailing north on July 25th. For once Napoleon was in two minds. His Foreign Minister, Talleyrand, convinced that he would have to face a superior British concentration in the Channel, was urging him not to risk a crossing. Yet the chance of destroying England, if not promptly taken, might pass for ever.

Then on the same day, August 8th, the Emperor learnt that Villeneuve had entered Vigo, claiming to have defeated Calder. He at once proclaimed a victory and sent him peremptory instructions to hurry north. Until the 13th his mind still seemed set on invasion. Then news arrived that Villeneuve, having reached Ferrol, had disregarded orders and entered the harbour. Beside himself with rage, Napoleon ordered an immediate military concentration against Austria. Yet, still hoping against hope, he dashed off letter after letter to Decrès and his errant admiral, exhorting the latter at all costs to put to sea, brush aside the British naval forces in his way and enter the Channel. 'The English,' he wrote, 'are not so numerous as you suppose. They are everywhere in a state of uncertainty and alarm. . . . Never did a fleet face danger for a grander object; never soldiers and seamen risk their lives for a nobler end. To destroy the Power which for six centuries had oppressed

France we can all die without regret.' Allemand, he added, was cruising off Ferrol, Ganteaume was waiting at Brest, the British had only four ships of the line in the Downs, and these were being harassed by French prames and gunboats. As for their main fleets, they were far away: Nelson and Collingwood were in the Straits, Cochrane in the West Indies, and others in the Indian Ocean. The plans to disperse them had succeeded: the army of invasion was waiting: only the Combined Fleet had still to fulfil its duty!

And on that very day, unknown to Napoleon, Villeneuve put to sea. No admiral ever sailed with a stronger sense of fear and doom. His ships were short of stores and water, their crews decimated by scurvy and dysentery, and the ill-trained Spaniards in a state of almost open mutiny. 'I will not venture to describe our condition,' he told the French Minister of Marine, 'it is frightful.'

For neither Villeneuve nor Gravina had the slightest belief in Napoleon's theory that half the British Navy was in the Antipodes. 'The plan of operations could not seem better,' the Spanish admiral wrote to Decrès, 'it was divine. But today it is sixty days since we left Martinique, and the English have had plenty of time to send warnings to Europe and to reinforce their Ferrol squadron. . . . It seems certain that on our leaving here they will give us battle and, by using scouts to warn their Ushant squadron, force a second fight on us before we can reach Brest.' For Gravina saw the false assumption in Napoleon's calculations: that a fleet could pass through the Western Approaches without being so mauled in the process as to be useless for further operations. Being a Spaniard, he felt free to point it out.

Before leaving Corunna Bay Villeneuve sent out a frigate to find Allemand, whose squadron had left

Rochefort in mid-July for a secret rendezvous with him off Finisterre. By a series of almost miraculous chances Allemand, though moving in waters swarming with British ships, had hitherto evaded detection and was at that moment cruising between Ushant and Finisterre in search of Villeneuve. But the latter's frigate never reached him. On August 10th she fell in with a slightly smaller English cruiser, provocatively disguised as a sloop, and, on attacking, was captured with all hands. By the time the Combined Fleet reached the open sea, Allemand, having no word of it and finding the enemy everywhere, had left his station and run for Vigo.

For what Allemand found all round him, and Villeneuve was sailing into the midst of, was the instinctive reaction of centuries. The British squadrons were assembling automatically in the very path that Napoleon had ordered the hapless Villeneuve to tread. On August 9th, discovering that the Combined Fleet had contacted the French and Spanish ships in Ferrol, Calder had raised the blockade and hastened northwards. On the 14th he joined Cornwallis off Ushant, a few hours after Rear-Admiral Stirling had also come in with his division. And at six o'clock next evening the Channel Fleet, already twenty-seven sail of the line including ten three-deckers, was joined by Nelson with twelve more. For learning on the 13th, while bound for his Scillies rendezvous, that Ireland was safe, that officer had at once altered course to bring his fleet to Cornwallis.

It was what Villeneuve most feared. 'Your Lordship each night forms a part of his dreams,' Captain Bayntun wrote to Nelson. It was an obsession that transcended ordinary reason. For as he hurried from sea to sea and port to port on his pitiful five months' mission, the French admiral felt he was struggling against more than ordinary mortal strength and ingenuity. In Nelson this honourable, brave but mediocre man had encountered one of the great elemental forces of nature. Being a Frenchman, he had the imagination to see it.

In such a mood he left the shelter of Corunna Bay on August 13th with twenty-nine sail of the line and ten cruisers. Of the former fourteen were Spanish. Only one, the *Principe de Asturias*, was a three-decker. The crews were largely made up of landsmen and soldiers. 'Our naval tactics,' Villeneuve wrote to Decrès, 'are antiquated, we know nothing but how to place ourselves in line, and that is just what the enemy wants.' The latter, he reported, was watching his every movement from the horizon; evasion was impossible. Forgetting his master's objurgation, he had already all but made up his mind to take his final option and seek refuge in Cadiz. For anything was better than to face the certain destruction lurking in the north.

Though he sailed on a north-easterly course, the French admiral never made any attempt to penetrate the British defences. At the first sight of a sail the entire fleet went about and continued on the opposite tack until the horizon was clear. Its only progress into the Bay was by night. Every hour, as it edged away from the dreaded north, it got farther into the west. There was no sign of Allemand; to reach Brest without a battle was impossible; at any moment Calder, and perhaps Nelson, might appear over the horizon. Far from dispersing the British the Grand Design, as Villeneuve had foreseen from the first, had concentrated them at the point where there was no avoiding them. A gale was blowing up from the north-east, his ships were ill-found, the soldiers and landsmen were seasick. As darkness fell on August 15th, he abandoned his enterprise and fled to Cadiz.

CHAPTER FIVE

TRAFALGAR

'To regard Trafalgar as having been fought
purely for the security of these British Islands is
to misjudge the men who designed it, and above
all, the men who fought it with such sure and
lucid comprehension. For them, from first to
last, the great idea was not how to avoid defeat,
but how to inflict it. England had found herself
again.'

Sir Julian Corbett,
The Campaign of Trafalgar

On August 18th 1805, Nelson anchored off Portsmouth
in the *Victory*. Having chased Villeneuve for 14,000
miles and failed to find him, he was depressed and
anxious about his reception. But the waiting crowds on
the ramparts were cheering, and all the way to the
capital the enthusiasm continued. Without knowing it
the tired, ailing Admiral had become a legend. Forgot-
ten during his long Mediterranean vigil and all but
reviled when the French fleet escaped from Toulon, his
dash to save the West Indies had caught the country's
imagination. Once more, as in the old days before his
passion for Lady Hamilton and his parting from his
wife had sullied his fame, he was 'our hero of the Nile'
—the wonderful Admiral whose name had swept
England's foes from the seas. The unexpected popularity was like sunshine to him. As he walked down
Piccadilly the people flocked about him : it was affect-
ing, wrote an eye-witness, to see the wonder, admiration
and love of every one, gentle and simple; 'it was beyond
anything represented in a play or a poem of fame.' The

West Indian merchants voted him thanks for having saved their possessions; but for his modesty, thought the *Naval Chronicle*, he was in danger of being turned into a demi-god.

The popular enthusiasm was partly the outcome of strain. Towards the end of July the fear of invasion had again become a reality: the enemy was known to be preparing feverishly on the opposite coast. Boulogne was reported packed with waiting barges: the Combined Fleet was at large and bound for the Channel. On August 10th the Admiralty warned Cornwallis that an attempt at a crossing was to be expected during the spring tides.

Since leaving the Bay on the 15th Villeneuve had never paused. Hurrying down the coasts of Galicia and Portugal, glimpsed momentarily by excited British frigates, he stopped only to capture and burn a solitary merchantman. Collingwood's 'three poor things with a frigate and a bomb' off Cadiz seemed utterly at his mercy. But, though sixteen capital ships were detached to destroy him, Collingwood evaded them. Resolved not to be driven through the Straits without dragging his pursuers after him and keeping just out of gunshot, he tacked whenever they tacked and finally, when their patience tired, followed them back to Cadiz. Meanwhile Calder, learning from a frigate that Villeneuve had left Ferrol with thirty battleships, also gave chase to the southward. 'It is a noble and most animating scene,' wrote Captain Codrington of the *Orion* to his wife, 'which I wish you could witness: eighteen sail of the line and but two frigates under every sail they can possibly set.' By the 29th they, too, were off Cadiz.

After seven months Napoleon's Grand Design had ended in humiliation and frustration. Only the prudence

or timidity of his admiral had saved his Fleet from a fate
as awful as that of the Spanish Armada. His Army, like
Parma's before it, was marooned on the shores of the
Channel with all hope of a crossing gone. The blockade
had been resumed. The Cadiz squadron was back in its
port and the Toulon and Ferrol squadrons blockaded
with it. Only Allemand's squadron was left at large—
its original purpose defeated. The initiative was again
beyond all dispute in British hands.

On the evening of September 2nd the *Euryalus*
frigate brought the news from Cadiz. As she heaved to
off the Needles Captain Blackwood went ashore to hire
a chaise and four in Lymington. At five in the morning
he stopped for a few minutes at Merton to see the most
famous man in England. He found him already up and
dressed. Like the rest of the world Nelson had been
eagerly awaiting the tidings he brought. 'Depend on it,
Blackwood,' he said, 'I shall yet give Mr. Villeneuve a
drubbing.' A few hours later he was receiving his charge
at the Admiralty from the First Lord. At his first return
Barham, who, scarcely knowing him, had distrusted his
brightly-coloured reputation, had sent for his journals.
But a few hours' perusal had resolved the old man's
doubts. Nelson might be a junior admiral and unortho-
dox, but he was complete master of his calling. His
right to return to his command—now of such supreme
significance—was indisputable.

Nelson received the summons with quiet gladness. 'I
hold myself ready to go forth whenever I am desired,'
he wrote to George Rose, 'although God knows I want
rest. But self is entirely out of the question.' His friends
had never seen him so cheerful. In those last quiet days
at Merton and in London, taking farewell of all he
loved, he radiated hope and inspiration.

While Napoleon, his hopes of invading England thwarted, was planning under the chestnuts of St. Cloud an immediate march of his army from Boulogne to the Danube to forestall the Austrian-Russian coalition which Pitt had mobilised against him, Nelson was bidding farewell to England. Much of his brief respite while the *Victory* was being made ready for sea he spent at the Admiralty, drawing up plans for his mission. Barham, who by now had completely surrendered to his fascination, offered him forty ships of the line and *carte blanche* to choose his officers. 'Choose yourself, my Lord,' the Admiral replied, 'the same spirit actuates the whole profession. You cannot choose wrong.'

Many saw him during those last days on his native soil. The painter, Haydon, watched him going into Dollond's near Northumberland House to buy a night glass—a diminutive figure with a green shade over one eye, a shabby, well-worn, cocked hat and a buttoned-up undress coat. Charles Lamb, who had formed a prejudice against him and thought him a mountebank, passed him in Pall Mall 'looking just as a hero should look'. The little Admiral 'with no dignity and a shock head' had captured the hearts of his countrymen at last: the challenging eye, the curving lip, the quick moods, the marks of exposure and battle struck deep into the popular imagination that autumn. Among those who met him was a young general, just returned from India who was waiting for an interview in the Secretary of State's ante-room. The famous Admiral, conspicuous by his empty sleeve and patch-eye, at first tried to impress him by his histrionic address. But after a few minutes, sensing something in his expression, Nelson left the room and, ascertaining from the porter that he had been talking to Arthur Wellesley, the victor of Assaye—and future Duke of Wellington—he returned and talked with him on public affairs with such good sense and knowledge that this most unimpressionable of men confessed he had never had a more interesting conversation.

Yet the real core of Nelson was his absolute self-surrender. 'I have much to lose and little to gain,' he wrote to his friend Davison, 'and I go because it's right, and I will serve the country faithfully.' The shy, austere Prime Minister, William Pitt, who shared the same unselfish love, showed his recognition of it when, on the Admiral's farewell visit to Downing Street, he waited on him to his carriage—an honour he would not have paid a Prince of the Blood.

At half-past ten on the night of Friday, September 13th, after praying by the bedside of his child, Horatia, Nelson took his leave of Merton. 'May the great God whom I adore,' he wrote in his diary, 'enable me to fulfil the expectations of my country.' Then he drove through the night over the Surrey heaths and Hampshire hills to Portsmouth. He spent the morning at the George Inn transacting business, and at two o'clock, accompanied by Canning and George Rose, who were to dine with him, went off to the *Victory*. Near the bathing machines, which he had chosen in preference to the usual landing stage, a vast crowd was waiting to see him go. 'Many were in tears,' wrote Southey, 'and many knelt down before him and blessed him as he passed. . . . They pressed upon the parapet to gaze after him when his barge pushed off, and he returned their cheers by waving his hat. The sentinels, who endeavoured to prevent them from trespassing upon this ground, were wedged among the crowd; and an officer, who had not very prudently upon such an occasion ordered them to drive the people down with their bayonets, was compelled speedily to retreat. For the people would not be debarred from gazing till the last moment upon the hero—the darling hero of England!'

On the following morning, Sunday the 15th, the *Victory* weighed, with the faithful Blackwood in attendance in the *Euryalus* frigate. All the way to the Scillies adverse weather continued; it was not till the 21st that the *Victory* cleared the Soundings. Then with a northerly wind she ran swiftly across the Bay and down the Portuguese coast. By September 25th Nelson was off Lisbon, sending an urgent warning to the British Consul to conceal his coming from the public, and another to Collingwood to refrain from hoisting colours on his arrival. 'For I hope,' he wrote, 'to see the enemy at sea.'

In the Fleet they were waiting for him a little wearily. After the excitements and disappointments of the summer the prospect of another winter of close blockade was having a depressing effect. 'These French rascals,' Captain Fremantle wrote, 'will never come out and fight but will continue to annoy and wear out both our spirits and constitutions. . . . Here I conclude we shall remain until Doomsday or until we are blown off the coast, when the Frenchmen will again escape us.' Some pinned their hopes on a peace through Russian mediation : few saw any prospect of ever seizing the elusive shadow, victory. To make matters worse, Collingwood, the acting Commander-in-Chief, shunned society and seldom communicated with anyone. He himself confessed in his letters home, that he was worn to a lath with this perpetual cruising : his sole comfort his dog Bounce and the thought of his home in Northumberland—'the oaks, the woodlands and the verdant meads.'

For it was only when the guns began to sound that Collingwood grew inspired. 'Is Lord Nelson coming out to us again?' asked Captain Codrington. 'I anxiously hope he may be that I may once more see a Commander-in-Chief endeavouring to make a hard and disagreeable service as palatable to those serving under him as circumstances will admit of and keeping up by his example that animation so necessary for such an occasion. . . . For charity's sake send us Lord Nelson, oh ye men of power!'

On September 28th the prayer was answered. As the *Victory* joined the Fleet the captains hurried aboard to greet the Admiral, forgetting everything in their enthusiasm. Their reception, Nelson told Lady Hamilton, caused the sweetest sensation of his life. 'He is so good and pleasant a man,' wrote Captain Duff on the *Mars*, a newcomer to his command, 'that we all wish to do what he likes without any kind of orders.' Codrington, who was also serving under him for the first time, spoke of the joy throughout the Fleet; everyone felt that his work would be appreciated and that nothing but the best would be good enough for such a commander. Soon every ship's company was busy painting in black and yellow bands after the old Mediterranean pattern and endeavouring to make her what the delighted Codrington called 'a dear Nelsonian—in all things perfect.'

For Nelson's task, as he made the Fleet aware, was to transform it into an instrument fit to do the service for which the country was waiting. Less than a third of its twenty-nine battleships had been with him in the Mediterranean. Of the remainder most, for all their companies' staunch virtues and wonderful skill, fell a little short of that flawless discipline, training and spirit which he expected of those who sailed with him. If he was to annihilate a superior enemy he knew he had to crowd into a few brief weeks, and perhaps only days, the teaching of years. And he had to school the captains, not of a mere squadron, but of the Navy itself, a third of whose fighting strength was now gathered under his command.

But Nelson in those autumn weeks of 1805 was a man exalted. On the two days after his arrival—the first of them his forty-seventh birthday—he entertained his flag officers and captains to dinner, and, as he laid before them his plans for destroying the enemy, an electric current ran through them.

Some who listened at the long table were strangers : others were old friends like Collingwood who had shared with him 'a brotherhood of more than thirty years'. But all were welded that night into one by the magic of the Nelson spirit and ritual : the gleaming silver and mahogany, the stately music, the cheerful, courtly hospitality, the friendliness and consideration, the sense which ran through all of sharing in a great adventure. Jealousy, sulking, backbiting—maladies that long confinement in overcrowded ships easily bred—could not survive in such an atmosphere. 'We can, my dear Coll, have no little jealousies,' Nelson wrote to his Second-in-Command. 'We have only one great object in view, that of annihilating our enemies and getting a glorious peace for our country.'

Consciously or unconsciously Nelson in those last weeks off Cadiz was fashioning a tradition and a legend which was to be of priceless service to England. He reminded the Navy that, whatever the bonds of authority, leadership was not a mere matter of transmitting orders but of evoking the will to serve. It was this which, as an officer said, double-manned every ship in the line. Nelson was essentially a humanitarian who, wooing men to duty, trusted them and had the imagination to see into their hearts. By his reckoning the best disciplinarian was he who most loved and understood men, who remembered that they were human and treated them accordingly. One of his first acts was to order that the names and families of all killed and wounded should be reported to him for transmission to the Chairman of the Patriotic Fund and that an account of every man's case should accompany him to hospital.

All the while that he was inspiring others with cheerfulness and resolution Nelson's own heart was aching for the home which he had barely seen and for the woman and child from whom he had so long been parted. On the second night after he entertained his captains to dinner he was seized by a painful and dreadful spasm. 'The good people of England will not believe,' he wrote, 'that rest of body and mind is necessary to me.' To comfort Emma, he told her that the brief days of happiness at Merton were only a foretaste of greater happiness : 'Would to God they were to be passed over again, but that time will, I trust, soon come, and many, many more days to be added to them.'

Even as he wrote he knew that what he had come to do precluded the probability of return. To secure his country and make her victory certain—whether now or in the more distant future—he had to destroy the great concentration lying before him in the inner harbour of Cadiz. The chance would probably never occur again and, when it came, a few brief hours of opportunity would be all he could hope to snatch from the gods of wind and tide. In that day with a force of less than thirty ships of the line—a few more, perhaps, if the promises given him in England could be made good—he

would have to shatter, burn and blast a superior enemy
fighting with the courage of desperation. Before him in
Cadiz were perhaps thirty-five or thirty-six sail of the
line including the three most powerful ships in the
world. At Cartagena, two days distant, were six more.
And to maintain his fleet on that inhospitable coast he
was under the necessity of sending it in detachments to
provision and water in the Straits. Almost his earliest
act had been to dispatch a first instalment of six battleships under Rear-Admiral Louis, thus reducing his fighting strength to twenty-three. 'I am very, very *very*
anxious,' he wrote to George Rose, begging for reinforcements. 'It is, as Mr. Pitt knows, annihilation the
Country wants and not merely a splendid victory of
twenty-three to thirty-six—honourable to the parties
concerned but absolutely useless in the extended scale
to bring Bonaparte to his marrow bones. Numbers only
can annihilate.'

For the menace created by the union of the French
and Spanish fleets still remained—a standing challenge
to England's strained resources. To keep the Grand
Fleet throughout the winter on that exposed and
treacherous shore was almost impossible. Yet at the least
easing of the blockade the enemy might escape either in
a body through the Straits, so imperilling the whole
Mediterranean position, or in detachments into the
Atlantic to harry trade and the colonies.

Still graver, in Nelson's view, was the risk of Villeneuve running for the Mediterranean. His statesman's
instinct warned him that Napoleon, having failed to
cross the Channel, would again, as in '98, turn eastwards
and try to conquer the world by breaking the ring of
British sea power at its weakest point—in the Levant.
His first step must be the great island off the toe of

Italy, which, still nominally ruled by the weak King of the Two Sicilies, was menaced by St. Cyr's army in the Calabrian ports. When Nelson left England no news had been received of the arrival at Malta of an expedition under General Craig which was to take part in an Anglo-Russian offensive in the Sicilian Straits. France and Russia were still nominally at peace and Austria, though mobilising, had not declared war. Yet the explosion might occur at any moment, and Nelson knew that when it did Napoleon would try to forestall the Allies in Sicily. That he would use Villeneuve and his great concentration at Cadiz to further his purpose seemed certain.

Nelson therefore withdrew his inshore squadron from before Cadiz and moved his fleet fifty miles out into the Atlantic where he could both guard against a surprise from the north and control the entrance to the Straits without the risk of being prematurely blown through them. The task of watching the enemy he left to Blackwood's frigates and a linking division of his faster seventy-fours, which maintained hourly communications by flag and gun signals. By withdrawing over the horizon he hoped to tempt Villeneuve out : everything, he told Blackwood, must yield to the overriding necessity of 'not letting the rogues escape without a fair fight.'

Unknown to the British, Villeneuve was already preparing for sea. On September 27th he had received Napoleon's order to sail for Cartagena and Naples. Anxious to recover his relentless master's esteem, he had at once ordered his captains to make ready. But on October 2nd, just as they were about to sail to 'strike down England's tyrannical dominion of the seas', rumours reached Cadiz of Nelson's arrival and of his plan to attack with infernal machines. Immediately the port was in a tumult; the order to sail was suspended and all hands were diverted to arming a harbour guard of gunboats. At a Council of War on October 7th, though an easterly breeze offered a chance of entering the Straits before the British could engage, it was resolved, after heated debate, to disobey Napoleon's orders. The French and Spanish admirals were brave men, but they had no wish to commit suicide. And to sail with Nelson in the offing, they reckoned, was suicide.

.   o   .

With Villeneuve's failure to use the east wind, hopes of a fight fell very low in the Fleet off Cadiz. Only Nelson, buoyed up by some inner sense of impending events, remained convinced that the enemy would put to sea. And on the very day that Villeneuve and his admirals were debating Napoleon's orders, Nelson's belief became a certainty. For the *Royal Sovereign* arrived from England after a refit with news that war had broken out in Europe and that Craig's army was on the point of leaving for Malta. The British Fleet, after securing the enemy in Cadiz, was ordered to cover his landing. Nelson now knew that Villeneuve or his successor would sail and what course he would take. The fate of Sicily, of the Mediterranean, of Pitt's new European coalition and, in the last resort, of England would be decided by a naval engagement at the mouth of the Straits.

For that ordeal—now imminent—Nelson summoned up all his art. The problem was to annihilate, for only annihilation would serve. Ever since he had learnt on that early September morning at Merton that Villeneuve had taken shelter in Cadiz he had been ponder-

ing how to destroy him. 'I will try to have a motto,' he
told Rose before he left England, 'or at least it shall be
my watchword—Touch and take !' He had never been
content with the classic conception of a naval victory :
an ordered cannonade in long, laboriously formed lines
of battle in which the French, receiving an attack from
windward were always able to withdraw, occasionally
leaving a few prizes in British hands. A disciple of the
great eighteenth century pioneers who had first had the
courage to defy the Admiralty's Fighting Instructions
and break the formal line of battle, and a lifelong
student of naval tactics, Nelson had long wrestled with
the problem of how to transform limited into decisive
victory. As a Commodore at Cape St. Vincent, and
then in his first independent command at the Nile, he
had pointed the way. But never till now had he directed
a major fleet in battle in the open sea.

On October 9th, two days after his new orders
reached him, he issued instructions to his flag officers
and captains. He had already outlined them verbally in
those two dramatic evenings in the *Victory*'s cabin. He
now committed them formally to writing. The problem,
as he saw it, was to bring such crushing force against a
portion of the enemy's line as to overwhelm it and to do
so in time to destroy the remainder before night fell.
'Thinking it almost impossible,' he wrote, 'to bring a
fleet of forty sail of the line into a line of battle in vari-
able winds, thick weather or other circumstances . . .
without such a loss of time that the opportunity would
probably be lost of bringing the enemy to battle in such
manner as to make the business decisive, I have made up
my mind . . . that the Order of Sailing is to be the Order
of Battle.' In other words, not only was the classical
line of battle to be discarded in the heat of the fight, as

E

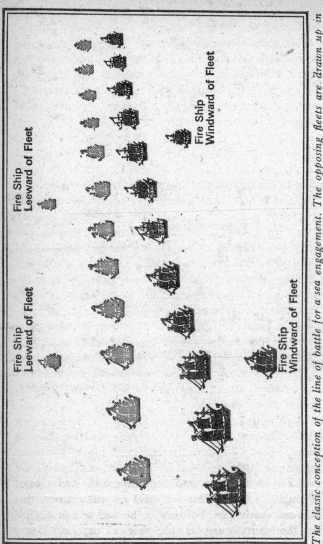

Fire Ship
Leeward of Fleet

Fire Ship
Leeward of Fleet

Fire Ship
Windward of Fleet

Fire Ship
Windward of Fleet

The classic conception of the line of battle for a sea engagement. The opposing fleets are drawn up in two parallel lines upon the wind. A comparison with the plan of the Battle of Trafalgar on page 138 will show how revolutionary was Nelson's plan of attack it had been in earlier engagements, but it was never to be formed at all.

The spirit of the offensive was implicit in every line of Nelson's Memorandum. So was his genius. Attack was to be made in two main divisions, one of which was to immobilise the enemy's van by a feint while the other broke and destroyed his rear and centre. No time was to be wasted in manoeuvring for position, for with the brief October days and the uncertain winds of that region none could be spared. Instead the approach was to be made by whatever course would most quickly bring the fleet to gunshot of the enemy's centre. Then one division under Collingwood was to break the enemy's line at about the twelfth ship from the rear, while the other, under Nelson's immediate command, after keeping the enemy's van in the maximum uncertainty as to its intentions by hovering to windward till it was too late to succour the rear, was to fall on the centre. 'The whole impression of the British Fleet,' Nelson wrote, 'must be to overpower from two or three ships ahead of their Commander-in-Chief, supposed to be in the centre, to the rear of their fleet. . . . I look with confidence to a victory before the van of the enemy can succour their rear.' Their flagship was to be taken, and the battle was not to be regarded as over so long as a single enemy ensign remained flying.

During the days that followed the issue of his Memorandum Nelson's main anxiety was lest the foe should escape through the Straits before his cruisers could warn him. As usual he was short of frigates : the last French fleet, he told the Admiralty, had slipped through his fingers that way and he was resolved that this one should not. Fortunately he had an apt disciple in the thirty-four-year old frigate captain, Henry

Blackwood. Much of his time, 'working like a horse in a mill' to complete the last detail of preparation, was spent in coaching this daring and vigilant officer. 'Those who know more of Cadiz than either you or I do,' Nelson wrote to him, 'say that after these Levanters come several days of fine weather, sea breezes westerly, land wind at night; and that, if the enemy are bound into the Mediterranean, they would come out at night, run to the southward and catch the sea breezes at the mouth of the Gut and push through whilst we might have little wind in the offing. In short, watch all points and all winds and weather, for I shall depend on you.'

Nelson was confident of his ability to defeat the enemy. 'I will give them such a shaking,' he told Blackwood, 'as they have never yet experienced; at least I will lay down my life in the attempt.' But he was growing increasingly anxious lest the reinforcements promised from England should not arrive in time to achieve complete annihilation. His lieutenant, Louis, with six of his battleships was still in the Straits, and he had now been forced by the needs of Malta and the Russians to send them farther eastward with a convoy past Cartagena. Others, however, despite the menace of Allemand to his supply lines, were straggling in as fast as Barham could dispatch them from the dockyards, and on the 13th the *Agamemnon* showed over the horizon with his old flag-captain, Berry, in command. 'Now we shall have a fight,' Nelson cried.

The newcomer brought the immediate strength under his flag to twenty-seven of the line including seven three-deckers. Yet the ships in Cadiz harbour continued to lie at their moorings, and Nelson began to wax impatient. 'I don't like to have these things on my mind,' he told a friend in England. On the 17th the wind veered into the east again : the Combined Fleet could not have finer weather for sea. But still there was no sign of life from the bare forest of masts beyond the low thin strip of the isthmus.

Yet within the port, unknown to the blockaders, the enemy was stirring. On October 11th, four days after the Council of War had decided not to fight, news arrived that Rosily was on his way to take over command and was already at Madrid. The idea of being superseded with a stigma of cowardice upon him was more than Villeneuve could bear. He knew that Louis was in the Straits : he did not yet know that reinforcements had arrived from England, for Nelson had been careful to conceal them. He therefore estimated British capital strength at twenty-three to his own thirty-three, with an equal number of three-deckers on either side. Of these one, the Spanish *Santissima Trinidad*, carried 130 guns, and two others 112 guns against the 100 guns of the largest British ships.

Reckoning that an occasion so favourable would never come again, Villeneuve ordered the fleet to sea. He would pass the Straits or perish. 'There is nothing,' he assured his captains, 'to alarm us in the sight of the English fleet; they are not more brave than we are, they are worn by a two years' cruise and they have fewer motives to fight well.' The chivalrous Spaniards, aware that more than half their crews had never been to sea, protested but, for the honour of their flag, agreed to sail. Villeneuve was now inexorable.

At six o'clock on the morning of Saturday, October 19th, the *Sirius*, Blackwood's nearest frigate inshore, gave the longed-for signal. 'Enemy have their topsail yards hoisted.' An hour later the first ships were reported coming out of the harbour. At half-past nine

Nelson received the news fifty miles out in the Atlantic. At once the signal was hoisted for a 'General Chase', followed soon afterwards by 'Prepare for Battle'. All day the British fleet stood towards the Straits under a clear sky with a north-easterly wind, intending to catch Villeneuve at the entrance to the Gut. Though during the afternoon the wind began to drop, the enemy's fleet was reported at sea. 'How would your heart beat for me, dearest Jane,' wrote Codrington to his wife, 'did you but know that we are now under every stitch of sail we can set, steering for the enemy.'

Yet by one o'clock on the morning of the 20th, when the fleet began to close on Gibraltar, there was no sign of the foe. Dawn broke on an empty solitude of thick, squally sea and cloud, with the fine weather of the previous day gone and, with it, Codrington's dream of a general engagement, a glorious victory and a quick return to England. 'All our gay hopes are fled,' he wrote, 'and instead of being under all possible sail in a very light breeze and fine weather, expecting to bring the enemy to battle, we are now under close-reefed topsails in a very strong wind with thick rainy weather and the dastardly French returned to Cadiz.' To add to the general disappointment there was no sign of Louis, whom Nelson had hoped to find in the Straits, that officer being now far away to the east, receding to his own intense chagrin and that of his crews in the direction of Malta.

Yet just as Nelson was about to beat back to his old station for fear of being driven by the south-wester through the Straits, word came from the frigates that Villeneuve was still at sea to the northward and that a group of his ships had just been sighted in some confusion off Cadiz lighthouse. The Combined Fleet's sea-

manship had proved unequal to the task of getting out
of the harbour in a single tide. But the ships were still
coming out. Nelson, therefore, after giving orders to
wear and stand to the north-west, called Collingwood
aboard for consultation. Yet, though he listened to his
eager advice to attack at once, he refused to do so. For,
if he was to gain the victory on which he counted, he
knew that he must let his foe get farther away from port.
He dared not trust his courage with a bolt-hole.

Later in the day, when the British fleet had reached a
point some twenty-five miles to the south-west of Cadiz,
there was an improvement in the weather, and visibility
became clearer. At one moment, owing to the continued
confusion of the enemy's ships—it was not till midday
that they were all clear of harbour—there was an alarm
that they were trying to get to the westward. But Nelson,
with his strong strategic grasp, refused to believe it,
especially as the wind was steadily shifting into the west.
He continued on his course, watching the enemy over
the rim of the horizon through the eyes of his frigates.
During the afternoon he spent some time on the poop
talking to his midshipmen; 'this day or tomorrow,' he
remarked, 'will be a fortunate one for you, young
gentlemen.' Later he entertained some of them at dinner,
promising that he would give them next day something
to talk and think about for the rest of their lives.

*   *

October 21st 1805 dawned calm and splendid. There
was a faint wind out of the west-north-west and a heavy
swell rolling in from the Atlantic towards Cape Trafalgar and the Gut of Gibraltar. The British fleet was
about twenty miles off the Spanish coast; the enemy

nine miles away to the south-east still steering towards
the Straits. The supreme moment of Nelson's life had
come. The whole horizon, clear after the low clouds of
yesterday, was filled with Villeneuve's ships.

Having summoned the frigate captains aboard, Nelson,
a little after six, gave the signal to form order of sailing
in two columns—his original idea of a third being
abandoned owing to his reduced numbers—and to bear
up and sail large on an east-north-easterly course, so
taking the fleet towards the enemy's line of retreat.
Shortly afterwards the signal 'Prepare for Action' was
made. An hour later the Admiral's prescience was justified, for Villeneuve, realising his adversary was more
powerful than he had supposed and fearful of meeting
Louis in the Straits, abandoned his course for the Gut
and gave the order to wear together and form line of
battle on the port tack in inverse order. But, though
by doing so he brought Cadiz under his lee, he was too
late to avoid an engagement.

Yet the enemy's movement added to Nelson's difficulties and the complexity of the attack. Not only was
the Combined Fleet sailing in inverse order, but his own
line of approach to it must now bring the shoals of
Trafalgar and San Pedro under his lee. And the heavy
ground swell and his seaman's instinct warned him that,
though at the moment the wind was dropping, a gale
from the Atlantic was imminent. When Blackwood came
aboard at eight o'clock to congratulate Nelson on his
good fortune, he found him, for all his cheerful spirits
and calm bearing, deeply intent on the enemy's direction and formation. The Admiral's thoughts were running, not on victory which he knew was by now
inevitable, but on the possibilities of the foe's escaping.
He told Blackwood to be ready to use his frigates in the

latter stages of the fight to complete the work of destruction and not to think of saving ships or men. For his end, he kept stressing, was annihilation, not prizes.

By this time the British fleet was approaching the enemy from windward, sailing to the eastward in two almost parallel lines at an oblique angle to his northerly course. Being in great confusion during and after its manoeuvre, the Combined Fleet was moving at a far slower pace, the van being forced to wait for the laggards, while the British leaders, with studding sails set on both sides, were forging ahead, leaving their own stragglers to follow as best they could. For both Nelson and Collingwood were resolved not to waste a minute of the all-too-short day, but to bring their ships to the attacking point by the shortest possible course.

There was little need for signals, for almost everything had been determined in advance. Collingwood's Lee Division which, in accordance with the Admiral's Memorandum, was to attack the enemy rear, was on a port line of bearing steering to cut the line at a point from twelve to sixteen ships ahead of the last ship. Nelson with the Weather Division was steering a slightly more northerly course towards the centre and—since the enemy's line was moving as well as his own—aiming at a point some two miles ahead of his leading ship. It was a wonderful sight, and Codrington in the *Orion* called up his lieutenants to see it : the Combined Fleet straggling like a forest of canvas across five miles of sea, its bright, many-coloured hulls, and the scarlet and white *Santissima Trinidad* towering up in the midst. Many of the enemy ships were doubling each other in their confusion and, instead of forming a straight line of battle, were tending to move in a wide crescent with its arc to leeward. By comparison the two British divisions, though

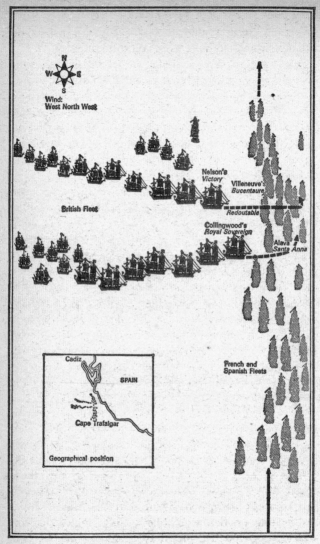

A plan of the opening stages of the Battle of Trafalgar

strung out a little in their haste, looked, with their black and yellow painted hulls, grim and forbidding.

About nine o'clock, with the fleets still several miles apart, Nelson made an inspection of the *Victory*. Dressed in his thread-bare, storm-stained admiral's frock-coat with the stars of his four Orders sewn on the left breast and accompanied by the frigate captains, he made the tour of the low, half-lit decks and the long curving lines of guns. The crews, stripped to the waists, waited with the alert silence of the Navy's age-long ritual, but here and there a whispered aside or a legend chalked on a gun revealed their mood. Walking swiftly, Nelson occasionally stopped to speak to the men at their quarters, repeating the old counsel that they were to hold their fire till they were sure of their object. Once he tapped a powder monkey on the shoulder and warned him to take off his shirt lest a spark should set it alight. Only when he reached the quarterdeck ladder to the poop did the pent-up emotion of the ship's company break in a great cheer. He stood there for a moment, with his emaciated figure and lined face, looking down on his men.

The wind was gradually failing and shifting into the west, and the pace of the British fleet slackened from three to two knots. But it was still gaining on the French and Spaniards who, from their thickening line and resolute bearing as they forged, close-hauled, slowly to the north-north-west, clearly meant to make a fight of it. Nelson from the poop watched them grimly, then observed, 'I'll give them such a dressing as they've never had before!' Blackwood, seeing that the flagship from her leading position would be unduly singled out for attack, suggested the propriety of letting one or two ships go ahead as was usual in line of battle. With a rather grim smile Nelson assented and ordered the *Temeraire* and *Leviathan* to pass the *Victory*. But, as the *Victory* continued to carry every stitch of sail she possessed, and as neither Captain Hardy nor Nelson would consent to shorten it, her consorts made little headway. Finally, as the *Temeraire* vainly struggled to pass, Nelson called out to her through his speaking-trumpet, 'I'll thank you, Captain Harvey, to keep in your proper station!' Thereafter the *Victory*, like the *Royal Sovereign* in the lee line, continued in indisputed possession of the lead. The order of sailing remained the order of battle.

About an hour before the time when the opposed lines seemed likely to converge, Nelson left the poop and retired to his dismantled cabin. Here Pasco, the flag-lieutenant, coming in with a message, found him on his knees composing the prayer which was part of his legacy to England:

'May the Great God whom I worship grant to my Country, and for the benefit of Europe in general, a great and glorious Victory; and may no misconduct in any one tarnish it; and may humanity after Victory be the predominant feature in the British Fleet. For myself, individually, I commit my life to Him who made me, and may His blessing light upon my endeavours for serving my Country faithfully. To Him I resign myself and the just cause which is entrusted to me to defend.'

Afterwards he made a codicil to his will, committing his child and Lady Hamilton to his country's keeping, and got Blackwood to witness it. Elsewhere, while the crew of the French flagship was taking a solemn oath to die with Villeneuve to the last man, other Britons were indulging in home thoughts. Captain Duff of the *Mars* scribbled a line to tell his wife that he was praying that he would behave as became him and still have the happiness of taking her and his children in his arms. Meanwhile, with the rich diversity of England, Codrington of the *Orion* was sitting down to a leg of turkey, and Cumby, the First Lieutenant of the *Bellerophon*, was piping the ship's company to dinner, 'thinking that Englishmen would fight all the better for a comfortable meal'.

Shortly after Nelson reappeared on the poop, land was sighted. At first, since the fleet had been sailing for several days on a dead reckoning, it was thought to be Cadiz, and the Admiral, fearful lest the enemy should escape, signalled that he would go through the end of the line to cut off their retreat. A few minutes later it was identified as Cape Trafalgar, and he reverted to his original plan. The *Victory* was now closing towards the centre of the enemy's van where the *Santissima Trinidad* and the French flagship, *Bucentaure*, towered up among their fellows. There was no desultory firing at long range, and it became plain that the enemy was holding himself in for a grim fight.

After signalling to make 'all possible sail', Nelson remarked to Pasco that he would amuse the fleet with a signal. 'I wish to say Nelson confides that every man will do his duty.' After a brief consultation about the capacity of Popham's code, this was altered to 'England expects'. Soon after it had been hoisted, and just as the first ranging shot from the *Fougueux* ploughed up the water in front of the *Royal Sovereign*, No. 16—'Engage the Enemy more closely'—was seen flying at the *Victory*'s masthead where it remained till it was shot away.

The advance was over: the battle about to begin. The British fleet had been brought in accordance with the terms of Nelson's Memorandum 'nearly within gun-shot of the enemy's centre'. The time had now come for the Lee Division to fall on his rear while Nelson prevented the van from coming to its aid. Judging that the disproportion of force and the enemy's inversed sailing order justified a modification of his original instructions, Collingwood decided to cut the line at the sixteenth instead of the twelfth ship from the rear. He thus set his fifteen battleships to engage not an inferior but a superior force. But he relied on British gunnery and discipline to give him the necessary ascendancy. Nelson approved, for as the *Royal Sovereign* bore down under a hail of fire on the great black hull of the *Santa Ana*, he cried out, 'See how that noble fellow Collingwood carries his ship into action!' His Second-in-Command, who, a few minutes before had been muttering, 'I wish Nelson would stop signalling; we know well enough what we have to do,' was now feeling the exaltation which always came to him in the hour of danger. Munching an apple like the countryman he was and pacing the quarter-deck as the shot splashed the water all round him, he remarked, 'Now gentlemen, let us do something today which the world may talk of hereafter.' What seemed to give him most delight was the resolute bearing of the French. 'No dodging and manoeuvring,' he wrote afterwards in ecstatic recollection. 'They formed their line with nicety and waited our attack with great composure. Our ships were fought with a degree of gallantry that would have warmed your heart. Everybody exerted themselves, and a glorious day they made it.'

The fight between the Lee Division and the enemy's rear began just before midday. At eight minutes past twelve, after enduring the fire of six French and Spanish ships for nearly a quarter of an hour, the *Royal*

Sovereign broke the line, discharging as she did so one broadside into the bows of the *Fougueux*. Then she ran alongside her, with the muzzles of the guns almost touching, and simultaneously engaged the *Indomptable* to leeward, evoking from the watching Nelson a slap of the thigh and a shout of, 'Bravo! Bravo! what a glorious salute!'

Five minutes later Collingwood's second ship, the *Belleisle*, followed the *Royal Sovereign* through the gap and ran abroad the *Fougueux*. Thereafter she took on seven ships in turn as they drifted by and, with her colours still flying at the stump of her shattered main-mast, ended by capturing a Spanish seventy-four. With-in a quarter of an hour eight of Collingwood's fifteen ships were in action, all breaking the line but the *Mars*, which lost her captain, Duff, at the first impact. At one moment no less than five enemy ships, fighting with the utmost gallantry, were pounding away at the *Royal Sovereign*, while Collingwood with his customary frugality helped one of his officers to take up an old studding-sail from the gangway hammocks and roll it up. But the terrific intensity of the British fire soon told: in three and a half minutes the *Royal Sovereign* dis-charged three broadsides. No ship, Collingwood had told his men, could stand up to three in five minutes, and he was proved right. 'A glorious day for old England!' he was heard to shout as the French rear began to crumple, 'we shall have one apiece before night.'

By now it was half-past twelve, and the *Victory* had opened fire on the enemy's centre. For the first half hour Nelson had been performing his essential task of con-taining and deceiving the French van while the Lee Division did its work. He had been steering to close with the *Santissima Trinidad*, the eleventh ship in the line,

meaning to break through between her and the
Bucentaure, two ships in rear. But while he did so he
retained his option of ranging up to the enemy's
advanced ships, keeping their flag-officer, Rear-Admiral
Dumanoir, in a state of impotent uncertainty till the
last possible moment. At one time he made a feint of
hauling out towards them, eliciting from Codrington the
tribute, 'How beautifully the Admiral is carrying his
design into effect!' Then, when it was too late for
Dumanoir to save the rear, he turned again to starboard and opened fire on the cluster of great ships in
the centre which he had marked as his special prey. At
this point he threw prudence to the winds and, bearing
up so as to pass under the lee of the *Bucentaure*, ran
straight at the enemy's line, bringing down upon the
Victory's bows the fire of hundreds of guns.

Because of the obtuse re-entering angle at which the
enemy's van was sailing, Nelson's approach, instead of
being oblique like Collingwood's, had of necessity far
more of the perpendicular in it than normal discretion
allowed. But, having served his primary purpose, his
object was now to get alongside the enemy as quickly
as possible and complete the work of destruction before
it was too late. He did so regardless of his own safety
and left the rest of his Division to scramble into the
fight as best it could. For, with the short October afternoon beginning to run, there was not a second to be lost.
As Blackwood left him to warn each captain to take
whatever course he thought fit to get quickly into
action, Nelson wrung his hand and bade him farewell.
'God bless you, Blackwood,' he said, 'I shall never speak
to you again.'

When Villeneuve saw the British flagship's sudden
turn he knew that his hour had come. Never, he wrote

after the battle, had he seen anything like the irresistible line of the British approach. But the final charge of the *Victory*, closely supported by the *Neptune* and *Temeraire*, was something he could not have conceived had he not actually witnessed it. It unnerved him. In sudden desperation he hoisted the signal for every ship not engaged to get into action without delay but failed to give the specific order to Dumanoir to tack and come to the aid of his encircled rear and centre. As a result the latter, still uncertain, continued to stand to the northward until it was too late to effect the course of the battle.

At 12.40 p.m. the *Victory*, within musket-shot of the French flagship, put her helm to port and steered for the stern of the *Bucentaure*. The line was at this point so close that the *Redoutable*'s jib boom was actually touching her leader's taffrail. Puzzled, the flag-captain asked the Admiral which of the two ships he should run down, only to receive the reply, 'Take your choice, Hardy, it does not much signify which.' As the *Victory* passed astern of the *Bucentaure* her mainyard, rolling with the swell, touched the vangs of the Frenchman's gaff; then with a terrific explosion her port broadside opened, while the forecastle carronade, raking the crowded deck, swept down a hundred of his crew. A moment later she ran aboard the *Redoutable* and broke the line. Behind her the *Temeraire*, *Neptune*, *Leviathan* and *Conqueror*, supported by *Britannia*, *Ajax* and *Agamemnon*, followed in quick succession.

By one o'clock the centre as well as the rear of the Franco-Spanish line was a mass of flame and billowing smoke. For nearly a mile between the two British flagships the ridge of fire and thunder continued. Codrington who, taking advantage of Nelson's order, had hauled out of line to starboard to reach the fight by the shortest route, calmly reserving his fire as he did so till he found an object worthy of it, described 'that grand and awful scene'—the falling masts, the ships crowded together, the broadsides crashing into blazing timbers at point blank range as rival boarding parties vainly sought an opportunity. For this was a sea battle of a pattern never previously attempted—more terrifying and more decisive. In the *Victory*, her mizen topmast shot away, her wheel broken, and her sails torn to shreds, the decks were swept continuously by rifle fire from the *Redoutable*'s tops, while every now and then a broadside from the *Bucentaure* or the *Santissima Trinidad* struck home with terrific force. A single shot killed eight marines on the poop. Another, narrowly missing Nelson, flung his secretary, a mangled heap of spurting blood, at his feet. 'This is too warm work, Hardy,' he said, 'to last long.' Down in the crowded cockpit the scene of horror was so awful that the chaplain, Scott, could bear it no longer and stumbled up the companion-ladder slippery with gore, for a breath of fresh air. There, 'all noise, confusion and smoke', he saw Nelson fall.

As they bore him down, his shoulder, lung and spine shot through and his golden epaulette driven deep into his body, the Admiral covered the stars on his breast with his blood-soaked handkerchief lest his men should see and be discouraged. 'They have done for me at last, Hardy,' he said. In the cockpit gasping from pain and exhaustion, he told the surgeon in broken sentences that he was past help. Five minutes later, as he lay there in the blinding darkness, the *Bucentaure*'s last mast fell, and Villeneuve, 'a very tranquil, placid, English-looking Frenchman, wearing a long-tailed uniform coat and green corduroy pantaloons,' sought for someone to whom he might surrender. A marine officer with five men from the *Conqueror* went aboard the French flagship to take him, while the British Admiral was being stripped of his clothes and covered with a sheet that the surgeon might probe his wound. As each French and Spanish ensign fluttered down, rounds of cheering broke from the *Victory*'s gundecks, faintly audible amid the cries and groans of the cockpit. 'It is nonsense, Mr. Burke,' Nelson whispered to the purser who bent over to fan him and give him water, 'to suppose that I can live. My sufferings are great but they will soon be over.'

By five minutes past two, little more than two hours after firing began, the action in the centre was all but done. Eight French and Spanish ships had been beaten out of the fight by five British, and, despite the heroism of their officers and crews, three after suffering appalling losses had been forced to surrender. About the same time, the *Santa Ana* struck to the *Royal Sovereign* in the Lee Division. Half an hour later the number that had yielded had increased to five, while seven more were isolated and doomed. To the north the ships of the French van were struggling, with the aid of rowing boats, to get round on the starboard tack, but remained cut off from the battle by the rear ships of Nelson's Division entering the fight from windward.

About this time, after repelling a last despairing attempt to board by the survivors of the shattered *Redoutable*, Hardy went below in response to the Admiral's repeated inquiries. He found him in great pain and weakness but with a mind still intent on the progress of the battle. 'I hope none of our ships have struck, Hardy,' he said when he had been told of his captures.

'No, my Lord, there is no fear of that!'

'I am a dead man, Hardy. I am going fast; it will be

all over with me soon. Come nearer to me. Pray let my dear Lady Hamilton have my hair and all other things belonging to me.'

About three-thirty the fight flared up again as Dumanoir's squadron stood down to rescue the last French and Spanish ships resisting in the centre and rear. But the *Victory*, calling a few undamaged consorts around her, barred the way. As her starboard guns opened fire, Nelson, clinging vainly to life, murmured, 'Oh, *Victory*, how you distract my poor brain!' Within twenty minutes the counter-attack had failed, and three more prizes had fallen to the British Weather Division. On this Hardy again went below and congratulated the Admiral on his victory, telling him that fourteen or fifteen enemy ships had surrendered. 'That is well,' whispered Nelson, 'but I had bargained for twenty.' Then the prescient mind of the great sailor, reverting to the thoughts of the morning and that steady, ominous swell out of the west, began once more to range ahead. 'Anchor, Hardy, anchor!' he cried with a sudden spasm of energy. Afterwards he begged the captain not to throw his body overboard, bade him take care of Lady Hamilton and his child, and, with some flash of childhood's tenderness battling against the delirium of pain, asked him to kiss him.

After Hardy had left, the Admiral began to sink fast. His voice became very low and his breathing oppressed. His mind now seemed to be running on his private life. 'Remember,' he told the chaplain, Scott, who was rubbing his chest to ease his pain, 'that I leave Lady Hamilton and my daughter Horatia as a legacy to my country.' 'I have *not*,' he said a minute later, 'been a *great* sinner, Doctor.' But towards the end he reverted to the battle, now dying around him. 'Thank God,' he kept repeating,

'I have done my duty.' The last words he said were, 'God and my Country.'

About the same time Dumanoir called off his four last uncaptured ships and hauled out of the fight. A quarter of an hour later the Spaniard Gravina, mortally wounded, hoisted the signal to retire and withdrew towards Cadiz with ten crippled ships, leaving the remainder in the victors' hands. As he did so, Nelson's spirit passed and became 'one with England and the sea'.

SELECT BIBLIOGRAPHY

Clarke, J. S. and McArthur, G.	*The Life of Admiral Lord Nelson* 1809
Conrad, J.	*Mirror of the Sea—Essay on Nelson* 1906
Corbett, Sir J.	*The Campaign of Trafalgar* 1905
Fenwick, K.	*H.M.S. Victory* 1959
Forester, C. S.	*Nelson* 1929
Grenfell, R.	*Nelson the Sailor* 1952
Howarth, D.	*Trafalgar, The Nelson Touch* 1969
Kennedy, L.	*Nelson's Band of Brothers* 1951
Kerr, Mark	*The Sailor's Nelson* 1932
Lobban, R. D.	*Nelson's Navy and the French Wars* 1968
Lord Barnham	*Letters and Papers of Lord Barnham* (Navy Records Society Vol III 1910)
Mahan, A. T.	*Life of Nelson* 1897
	Influence of Sea Power upon the French Revolution and Empire 1892
Manwaring, J. and Dobrée, B.	*The Floating Republic* 1935
Masefield, J.	*Sea Life in Nelson's Time* 1905
Nicolas, Sir H.	*The Despatches and Letters of Vice-Admiral Lord Nelson* 1844–6

Oman, C.	*Nelson* 1947
	Lord Nelson 1968
Pocock, T.	*Nelson and His World* 1968
Pugh, P. D. G.	*Nelson and His Surgeons* 1968
Rawson, G.	*Nelson's Letters* 1960
Richardson, P.	*Nelson's Navy* 1967
Robinson, C. N.	*The British Sailor in Fact and Fiction* 1909
Russell, J.	*Nelson and the Hamiltons* 1969
Southey, R.	*Life of Nelson* 1813
Thursfield, J. R.	*Nelson and Other Naval Studies* 1909
Warner, O.	*A Portrait of Lord Nelson* 1958
	Battle of the Nile 1960
	Trafalgar 1959
	Nelson and the Age of Fighting Sail 1963

LIST OF ILLUSTRATIONS

INDEX